teach yourself ®

quick fix
german grammar
susan ashworth-fiedler

For over 60 years, more than
40 million people have learnt over
750 subjects the **teach yourself**
way, with impressive results.

be where you want to be
with **teach yourself**

For UK order enquiries: please contact Bookpoint Ltd, 130 Milton Park, Abingdon, Oxon OX14 4SB. Telephone: +44 (0) 1235 827720. Fax: +44 (0) 1235 400454. Lines are open 09.00–18.00, Monday to Saturday, with a 24-hour message answering service. Details about our titles and how to order are available at www.teachyourself.co.uk

For USA order enquiries: please contact McGraw-Hill Customer Services, PO Box 545, Blacklick, OH 43004-0545, USA. Telephone: 1-800-722-4726. Fax: 1-614-755-5645.

For Canada order enquiries: please contact McGraw-Hill Ryerson Ltd, 300 Water St, Whitby, Ontario L1N 9B6, Canada. Telephone: 905 430 5000. Fax: 905 430 5020.

Long renowned as the authoritative source for self-guided learning – with more than 40 million copies sold worldwide – the **teach yourself** series includes over 300 titles in the fields of languages, crafts, hobbies, business, computing and education.

British Library Cataloguing in Publication Data: a catalogue record for this title is available from the British Library.

Library of Congress Catalog Card Number: on file.

First published in UK 2003 by Hodder Education, 338 Euston Road, London, NW1 3BH.

First published in US 2003 by Contemporary Books, a division of the McGraw-Hill Companies, 1 Prudential Plaza, 130 East Randolph Street, Chicago, IL 60601 USA.

The **teach yourself** name is a registered trade mark of Hodder Headline.

Typeset by Transet Limited, Coventry, England.
Printed in Great Britain for Hodder Education, a division of Hodder Headline, 338 Euston Road, London NW1 3BH, by Cox & Wyman Ltd, Reading, Berkshire.

Hodder Headline's policy is to use papers that are natural, renewable and recyclable products and made from wood grown in sustainable forests. The logging and manufacturing processes are expected to conform to the environmental regulations of the country of origin.

Impression number   10 9 8 7 6 5 4 3
Year   2007 2006 2005

contents

Abbreviations used in this book

nom.	nominative	*m./masc.*	masculine
acc.	accusative	*f./fem.*	feminine
gen.	genitive	*nt.*	neuter
dat.	dative	*pl.*	plural

Teach Yourself Quick Fix German Grammar makes German grammar interesting and easy. It is a reference and practice book for elementary learners of German. It will also be useful for anyone who feels they need more practice of basic German grammar structures. The book offers you 90 units of clear grammar explanations and simple examples followed by exercises, with a **more practice** section at the back of the book.

How to use the book

Decide which grammar point you are going to practise. You need not work through the book from beginning to end. Use the **contents list** at the beginning of the book and/or the **index** at the end to find the unit(s) you would like to look at. Start by reading the explanations and examples, then do the exercises that follow. You will find a useful **vocabulary list** on pp. 241–4. Use the **keys** at the back of the book to check your answers. If you have difficulties with an exercise, look at the explanations and examples again.

The explanations are as simple as possible but some grammatical terms ('verb', 'tense', 'case', etc.) are used. You can look at the **glossary** on pp. 235–40 for more information on these terms. Use the final three units of the book for easy reference. They contain useful lists of verbs and tenses and revision tables.

Viel Spaß!

introduction

Nouns are words used to name people, things, places and ideas. Gender indicates whether a noun is masculine, feminine or neuter.

A In German, nouns are divided into three groups known as *genders*: masculine, feminine or neuter. Each group has a different word for *the*: **der**, **die** or **das**.

masculine	feminine	neuter
der Computer *the computer*	die Lampe *the lamp*	das Büro *the office*

The is known as the definite article.

B All nouns start with a capital letter in German: das Buch *the book*, der Hund *the dog*.

C It is easy to work out the gender of some words: male persons are masculine: **der Junge** (*the boy*) and female persons are feminine: **die Frau** (*the woman*). If you do not know the gender of a noun, you can look it up in a dictionary. The gender of each noun appears after the word. Note that the abbreviations *m.* (masculine), *f.* (feminine) and *nt.* (neuter) are usually used.

Küche (f.) *kitchen* → **die** Küche
Garten (m.) *garden* → **der** Garten
Wohnzimmer (nt.) *living room* → **das** Wohnzimmer

D In German, there are also three genders of *a(n)* (the indefinite article): **ein**, **eine** and **ein**.

masculine	feminine	neuter
ein Bahnhof *a railway station*	eine Post *a post office*	ein Museum *a museum*

masculine	feminine	neuter	
der	die	das	*the*
ein	eine	ein	*a(n)*

exercises

1 Say whether these nouns are masculine (der), feminine (die) or neuter (das).

E.g. Haus → das Haus

a Junge

b Lampe

c Garten

d Küche

e Museum

2 Put in the correct indefinite article (ein, eine or ein) in front of each noun.

E.g. Tankstelle (f.) → eine Tankstelle

a Hotel (nt.)

b Kirche (f.)

c Supermarkt (m.)

d Krankenhaus (nt.)

e Bäckerei (f.)

f Theater (nt.)

These general guidelines will help you to work out the gender of some nouns from their endings.

A The following endings usually indicate masculine nouns which take **der/ein:**

-er	der Wecker *alarm clock*	-ig	der König *king*
-ich	der Teppich *carpet*	-or	der Motor *engine*
-ling	der Frühling *spring*		
-iker	der Informatiker *computer scientist*		

B The following endings usually indicate feminine nouns which take **die/eine:**

-age	die Garage *garage*	-ik	die Politik *politics*
-e	die Woche *week*	-ei	die Metzgerei
-ette	die Toilette *toilet*		*butcher's*
-heit	die Gesundheit *health*	-ion	die Religion *religion*
-keit	die Schwierigkeit *difficulty*		
-schaft	die Freundschaft *friendship*		
-ung	die Wohnung *apartment*		
-in	die Floristin *female florist*		

C **-in** is often added to the masculine form for female job titles and nationalities.

der Lehrer *male teacher* → die Lehrerin *female teacher*
der Schweizer *Swiss man* → die Schweizerin *Swiss woman*

D The following endings usually indicate neuter nouns which take **das/ein:**

-chen	das Mädchen *girl*	-o	das Kino *cinema*
-lein	das Fräulein *Miss*	-um	das Zentrum *centre*
-ma	das Thema *theme, topic*		
-ment	das Dokument *document*		

exercises

1 Add the definite article der (m.), die (f.) or das (nt.) then underline the odd one out in each group.

E.g. _____ Wecker, _____ Teppich, _____ Wohnung, _____

Fernseher → der Wecker, der Teppich, <u>die Wohnung</u>, der Fernseher

a _____ Zentrum, _____ Auto, _____ Dokument, _____ Motor
b _____ Datum, _____ Mädchen, _____ Karte, _____ Museum
c _____ Büro, _____Ordner, _____ Informatiker, _____ Computer
d _____ König, _____ Tante, _____ Studentin, _____ Königin

2 Add the correct article (ein, eine or ein) in front of each noun and write down the English meaning for each word.

E.g. _____ Pullover → *ein* Pullover (*a pullover*)

a _____ Bäckerei
b _____ Album
c _____ Kino
d _____ Woche
e _____ Radio
f _____ Garage
g _____ Freundschaft
h _____ Zentrum
i _____ Religion
j _____ Wohnung

Certain groups of words have the same gender. For example, days of the week are all masculine and most place names are neuter.

A The following groups of nouns are all masculine and take **der/ein**.

- male persons: der Junge *boy*; der Arzt *doctor*; der Italiener *Italian*
- large male animals: der Bär *bear*
- days: der Montag *Monday*
- months: der Juni *June*

- seasons: der Sommer *summer*
- points of the compass: der Süden *south*
- alcoholic drinks: der Wein *wine*
- makes of cars: der Mercedes *Mercedes*

Exceptions are **das Baby** (*baby*), **das Bier** (*beer*)

B The following groups are usually neuter and take **das/ein**.

- young persons: das Baby *baby*
- young animals: das Küken *chicken*
- place names: das Berlin *Berlin*
- continents: das Europa *baby*

- countries: das Deutschland *Germany*
- cinema names: das Astori *Astoria*
- hotel names: das Columbi *Columbi*
- metals: das Silber *silver*
- materials: das Holz *wood*

Exceptions are **die Schweiz** *Switzerland*, **die Vereinigten Staaten** *the United States*, **die Türkei** *Turkey*, **die Bronze** *bronze*.

exercises

1 One of the nouns in each of the following groups has a different gender. Put in the genders of the nouns and underline the odd one out.

E.g. _____ Westen, _____ Küken, _____ Sommer →
   der Westen, <u>das Küken</u>, der Sommer

a _____ Wein, _____ Bier, _____ Whisky
b _____ Junge, _____ Mann, _____ Baby
c _____ Küken, _____ Bär, _____ Lamm
d _____ Gold, _____ Silber, _____ Bronze

2 Fill in the indefinite article (ein) and indicate whether the noun is masculine (m.) or neuter (nt.).

E.g. Direktor → ein Direktor (*m.*)

a Elefant
b Arzt
c Wein
d Bier
e Winter
f Baby

Certain groups of nouns are feminine (die) words. In German, there is a feminine form for job titles, nationalities and animals.

A The following groups are usually feminine and take **die/eine**.

- female persons: die Mutter *mother*
- small animals: die Ente *duck*
- flowers: die Tulpe *tulip*
- trees: die Tanne *fir*
- rivers: die Themse *Thames*
- numerals: die Eins *one*
- ships: die Titanic *Titanic*
- planes: die Concorde *Concorde*

Exceptions are nouns ending in -chen + -lein: **das Mädchen** *girl*, **das Fräulein** *Miss, young woman* and some rivers: **der Rhein** *Rhine*, **der Main** *Main*.

B The feminine form of job titles, nationalities and some female animals is formed by adding **-in** ending to the masculine form of the noun. If the masculine noun ends in **-e**, take off the final **-e**. An umlaut is usually added to the vowel (**ä, ö, ü**) if there isn't one already.

der Arzt →	die Ärztin *the male/female doctor*
der Lehrer →	die Lehrerin *the teacher*
der Schotte →	die Schottin *the Scotsman/woman*
der Engländer →	die Engländerin *the Englishman/ woman*
der Löwe →	die Löwin *the lion/lioness*

Not all female equivalents are formed in this way.

der Geschäftsmann → **die Geschäftsfrau**
businessman/woman

exercises

1 Give the opposite gender form of these nationalities and put in the correct article.

E.g. die Schottin → der Schotte

a Spanierin
b Französin
c Italiener
d Engländerin
e Norweger
f Amerikanerin
g Grieche

2 What is the feminine form of these professions?

E.g. der Tierarzt → die Tierärztin

a der Arzt
b der Polizist
c der Zahnarzt
d der Koch
e der Architekt
f der Geschäftsmann
g der Lehrer

Compound nouns are made up of several words which are written as one word.

A Compound nouns are words formed by joining two or more nouns together.

> das **Auto** *car* + die **Bahn** (*track*) → die **Autobahn** *motorway*
> der **Markt** *market* + der **Platz** *square* → der **Marktplatz** *market square*

B The compound noun takes its gender from the last part of the word.

> **das** Taxi + **der** Fahrer → **der** Taxifahrer *taxi driver*
> **der** Kaffee + **die** Kanne → **die** Kaffeekanne *coffee pot*
> **der** Kopf + **das** Kissen → **das** Kopfkissen *pillow*

C You sometimes need to add an extra letter to the end of the first noun when joining two nouns together. When the first word ends in **-e** you usually add an extra **-n**.

> die Blume + das Geschäft → das Blume**n**geschäft *flower shop*
> die Woche + das Ende → das Woche**n**ende *weekend*

Some nouns are formed by adding another word at the front. This word is known as a *prefix*. For example the prefix **Haupt** means *main*.

> der Bahnhof *station* → der **Haupt**bahnhof *main station*
> die Stadt *town, city* → die **Haupt**stadt *capital city*
> die Post *post office* → die **Haupt**post *main post office*

D Some nouns add another word at the end. This word is known as a *suffix*.

For example, the suffix -ei is used with feminine nouns for places of work.

> der Bäcker *baker* → die Bäckerei *baker's*
> der Metzger *butcher* → die Metzgerei *butcher's*
> der Konditor *pastry-cook* → die Konditorei *cake shop*

exercise

1 Build new words and add the correct article (der, die or das).

E.g. **das Bier + der Garten → *der Biergarten***

a die Stadt + der Plan
b das Telefon + das Buch
c der Kaffee + die Maschine
d der Fußball + das Stadion
e der Tee + die Kanne
f das Gold + der Fisch
g die Tomate + die Suppe
h die Schokolade + das Eis

Abbreviations are short forms for names, titles, etc., such as der ADAC. Some nouns have more than one gender, e.g. der/das Curry.

A Abbreviations take their gender from the main word.

die SPD → die Sozialdemokratische Partei Deutschlands
the Social Democratic Party of Germany
der ADAC → der Allgemeine Deutsche Automobil-Club
the General German Automobile Club

B Some nouns have more than one gender but their meanings stay the same.

der/das Curry *curry*
der/das Bonbon *sweet*
der/das Cartoon *cartoon*

der/das Joghurt *yoghurt*
der/das Keks *biscuit*
der/das Liter *litre*

C Some nouns have different genders for different meanings.

der See *lake*
der Band *volume/book*
das Band *ribbon, tape*
das Golf *golf*
der Leiter *leader*
der Messer *gauge*
der Pony *fringe (hair)*
die Steuer *tax*

die See *sea*
die Band *band, pop group*

der Golf *Gulf*
die Leiter *ladder*
das Messer *knife*
das Pony *pony*
das Steuer *steering wheel*

exercise

1 Match each word to a picture and add the correct article.

| Band | ~~See~~ | Golf | Leiter | Keks | Pony | Messer |

E.g.

der See

a

b

c

d

e

f

When you talk about more than one thing, you use the plural. In German, there are several different plural forms for nouns.

A der Schuh → **die Schuhe**   *the shoes*
  der Mann → **zwei Männer**   *two men*

B The plural form of **der, die** and **das** is **die**.
  der Finger → **die** Finger   *the fingers*
  die Torte → **die** Torten   *the cakes*
  das Haus → **die** Häuser   *the houses*

C The vowel sometimes takes an umlaut in the plural (ä, ö, ü).
  der Zahn → die Zähne   *the teeth*
  der Baum → die Bäume   *the trees*
  die Nuss → die Nüsse   *the nuts*
  der Koch → die Köche   *the chefs*

D If you do not know the plural of a noun, you can look in a dictionary. The plural form is given after the noun and gender.
Hund (m.) (-e) → der Hund → die Hunde *the dogs*
Dorf (nt.) (⸚er) → das Dorf → die Dörfer *the villages*

Here are some guidelines for the plural endings of masculine nouns.

	plural ending	singular	plural	meaning
many nouns add	-e	der Tag	die Tage	*days*
some nouns add	⸚e	der Sohn	die Söhne	*sons*
some nouns add	-en	der Mensch	die Menschen	*people*
some nouns add	⸚er	der Mann	die Männer	*men*
nouns ending in: -er, -el, -en	–	der Kellner	die Kellner	*waiters*

exercises

1 Write out the nouns in the plural form by using the endings in brackets.

E.g. der Tisch (-e) → die Tische

a der Fisch (-e)
b der Pullover (–)
c der Bruder (⸚)
d der Student (-en)

e der See (-n)
f der Monat (-e)
g der Kuchen (–)

2 Are the nouns in the singular or plural? Underline the correct form of the verb.

E.g. Die Hunde spielt/<u>spielen</u>.

a Die Männer wohnen/wohnt in Hildesheim.
b Der Kellner arbeitet/arbeiten im Restaurant Landhaus.
c Die Schuhe ist/sind rot.
d Die Bücher liegt/liegen auf dem Tisch.

Feminine nouns (die words) and neuter nouns (das words) form their plurals in various ways.

A die Tomate, **die** Tomaten *tomatoes*; das Bild, **die** Bilder *pictures*

B Here are some guidelines for the plural endings of feminine nouns.

feminine	plural ending	singular	plural	meaning
most nouns	-en	die Frau	die Frauen	*women*
some nouns	̈e	die Hand	die Hände	*hands*
nouns ending in -e	-n	die Straße	die Straßen	*streets*
job titles	-nen	die Lehrerin	die Lehrerinnen	*teachers*
nationalities	-nen	die Spanierin	die Spanierinnen	*Spanish women*

C Here are some guidelines for the plural endings of neuter nouns.

neuter	plural ending	singular	plural	meaning
many nouns	-e	das Bein	die Beine	*legs*
some nouns	̈er	das Bad	die Bäder	*baths*
nouns ending in -chen, -lein	–	das Mädchen	die Mädchen	*girls*

D Other plural forms include names of families, which take -s, and foreign words, which also take -s.

plural	plural ending	plural	meaning
family names	-s	die Beckers	the Beckers
foreign words	-s	die Hotels	hotels

exercises

1 Underline the plural nouns.

E.g. Die <u>Müllers</u> wohnen in Baden-Baden.

a Die Schmidts wohnen in Köln.

b Sie haben drei Kinder – zwei Söhne und eine Tochter.

c Die Autos sind in der Garage.

d Frau Schmidt und ihre Tochter sind beide Lehrerinnen.

e Die Söhne arbeiten im Krankenhaus.

2 Write these nouns in the plural.

E.g. das Haus → die Häuser

a das Mädchen _____

b die Italienerin _____

c die Straße _____

d das Bad _____

e die Frau _____

f die Sekretärin _____

g das Hotel _____

In German, masculine and feminine nouns of nationality take different endings.

A Like other masculine nouns, some masculine nouns of nationality only take an ending in the genitive singular and dative plural forms.

der Engländer → **des** Engländers (gen. / sing.); **den** Engländern (dat. / pl.)

These masculine nouns follow the same pattern:

der Afrikaner *African*	der Italiener *Italian*
der Australier *Australian*	der Norweger *Norwegian*
der Amerikaner *American*	der Österreicher *Austrian*
der Belgier *Belgian*	der Schweizer (*Swiss man*)
der Holländer *Dutchman*	der Spanier *Spaniard*

Er ist Amerikaner.   *He's American.*

B Some masculine nouns of nationality take weak noun endings. They always add an -(e)n ending except in the nominative singular form.

Der Schotte (nom.) arbeitet in Glasgow. *The Scotsman works in Glasgow.*

Ich kenne einen Schotten (acc.).   *I know a Scotsman.*

These masculine nouns follow the same pattern:

der Brite *Briton*	der Ire *Irishman*
der Däne *Dane*	der Portugiese *Portuguese*
der Finne *Finn*	der Russe *Russian*

der Franzose *Frenchman*   der Schwede *Swede*
der Grieche *Greek*   der Ungar *Hungarian*

Der Franzose wohnt in Paris.   *The Frenchman lives in Paris.*

der/die Deutsche *the German man/woman* take adjective endings.

To form feminine nouns of nationality, add **-in** for the singular and **-innen** for the plural to the masculine (nom.) form.

die Engländer**in** *the Englishwoman* → die Engländer**innen**
die Französ**in** the Frenchwoman → die Französ**innen**

exercise

1 Who lives in these countries? What nationality are they?

E.g. Norwegen → Er ist Norweger. Sie ist Norwegerin.

a Portugal
b Großbritannien
c Schottland
d Österreich
e Italien
f Frankreich
g Spanien
h Griechenland
i Afrika
j USA
k Norwegen
l Belgien

In German, the article (der, ein, etc.) is used before most nouns. The article is sometimes omitted in German but not in English and vice versa.

A The following categories of nouns are preceded by an article.

- Time expressions with a preposition
  im (= in dem) Winter/Sommer *in winter/summer*
  am (= an dem) Samstag *on Saturday*

- Seasons
  Der Frühling fängt im April an. *Spring starts in April.*

- Meal times
  Das Mittagessen ist um ein Uhr. *Lunch is at one o'clock.*
  Das Frühstück ist um sieben Uhr. *Breakfast is at seven.*

B The following categories don't take an article in German.

- Professions
  Er ist Programmierer. *He is a programmer.*
  Sie ist Krankenschwester. *She is a nurse.*

- Instruments
  Tobias spielt Klavier. *Tobias plays the piano.*

- Expressions with haben
  Ich habe Kopfschmerzen/Halsschmerzen. *I've got a headache/ a sore throat.*

C There is no article in German in the following expressions where *some* or *any* is used in English.

Ich habe Geld. *I've got **some** money.*

Haben Sie Karten? *Have you got **any** tickets?*

exercises

1 Say what he or she does as a profession. Translate into English.

E.g. Er/Taxifahrer → Er ist Taxifahrer. → *He is a taxi driver.*

a Sie/Friseurin

b Er/Koch

c Sabine/Krankenschwester

d Herr Schmidt/Geschäftsmann

2 What's the matter? Translate the phrases into German.

a She's got toothache.   c She's got backache.

b He's got stomachache.   d He's got a sore throat

3 Put in the article where necessary.

E.g. _____ Frühstück ist um acht Uhr. →

Das Frühstück ist um acht Uhr.

a In _____ Winter fahren wir Ski.

b Wir haben _____ Tomaten.

c _____ Abendessen ist um 20.00 Uhr.

d Haben Sie _____ Geld?

e Stefan spielt _____ Gitarre.

f Maria ist _____ Spanierin.

There are four cases in German. Cases show the role that nouns play in a sentence. The articles der, die, das (the) and ein, eine, ein (a(n)) change according to the case.

Die Band spielt Musik.
The band is playing music.

A The nominative case of the article is the form you find in the dictionary.

der Tisch (*m.*)	*the table*
die Katze (*f.*)	*the cat*
das Buch (*n.*)	*the book*

B The nominative case shows the subject of the sentence. The subject is the person or thing that does the action of the verb.

subject	verb	object	
Der Mann	trinkt	ein Bier.	*The man is drinking a beer.*
Die Frau	schreibt	eine Geburtstagskarte.	*The woman is writing a birthday card.*
Das Kind	isst	den Keks.	*The child is eating the biscuit.*

C If you want to say *a* rather than *the*, you use **ein**, **eine** or **ein** in German.

Ein Mann arbeitet im Büro.   *A man is working in the office.*
Eine Frau kauft eine Jacke.   *A woman is buying a jacket.*

D The subject is not always at the beginning of the sentence.

Nach der Schule geht **das**   *After school the girl*
   Mädchen nach Hause.   *goes home.*

E Here is a summary of the articles in the nominative case.

m.	f.	nt.	pl.	
der	die	das	die	*the*
ein	eine	ein	keine*	*a(n)*

*As there is no plural form of **ein**, the negative **keine** *no, not any* is included in the plural.

exercise

1 Underline the subject (the word in the nominative case) in each sentence.

E.g. <u>Die Kinder</u> spielen auf dem Spielplatz.

a Der Arzt arbeitet in der Stadt.
b Der Hund spielt im Garten.
c Die Frau hat das Kind gesehen.
d Am Abend geht der Mann ins Kino.
e Das Auto steht in der Garage.
f Das Haus ist in der Kreuzstraße.

The direct object of a sentence is in the accusative case.

A The accusative case is used for the direct object. The direct object is the person or thing that has the action done to it.

subject	verb	direct object	
Ich	trinke	**den Wein.**	*I am drinking the wine.*
Susi	trägt	**die Tasche.**	*Susi is carrying the bag.*
Georg	wäscht	**das Auto.**	*Georg is washing the car.*

B The following table summarizes the articles in the nominative and accusative case endings.

	the				a(n)			
	m.	f.	nt.	pl.	m.	f.	nt.	pl.
nom.	der	die	das	die	ein	eine	ein	keine
acc.	**den**	**die**	**das**	**die**	**einen**	**eine**	**ein**	**keine**

The nominative and accusative cases only differ in the masculine form.

Doris hat **einen Bruder.**   *Doris has a brother.*
Ich möchte **eine Cola.**   *I'd like a coke.*
Wir haben **ein Zimmer** reserviert. *We've booked a room.*

C The accusative case is also used in certain expressions of time, measurement and distance.

Ich war **einen Monat** in Rom. *I was in Rome for a month.*
Die Post ist **einen Kilometer** *The post office is a kilometre*
von hier. *from here.*

D Some prepositions are followed by the accusative.
Wir gehen **durch den Park**. *We are going through the park.*

Wir gehen morgen Abend **ins** *We are going to the cinema*
(in das) **Kino**. *tomorrow evening.*

exercise

1 You have moved house and want to buy new furniture.
Make sentences beginning with: **Ich möchte ...** (I'd like ...)
and the accusative form of **ein**.

E.g. eine Waschmaschine →
Ich möchte eine Waschmaschine kaufen.

a ein Tisch (m.)
b ein Sofa (nt.)
c ein Herd (m.)
d eine Lampe (f.)
e ein Stuhl (m.)
f ein Bett (nt.)
g eine Spülmaschine (f.)
h ein Kleiderschrank (m.)

The dative case shows the indirect object of the sentence. The indirect object is the person or thing that is shown, told, etc. something.

A In German, the dative case endings make it clear who or what is the indirect object in the sentence. In English, *to* is often used with the indirect object.

subject	verb	indirect object	direct object	
Ich	zeige	**dem Mann**	das Foto.	*I show the man the photo./ I show the photo to the man.*

B The following table summarizes the articles in the nominative and dative cases.

	m.	f.	nt.	pl.	m.	f.	nt.	pl.
nom.	der	die	das	die	ein	eine	ein	keine
dat.	dem	der	dem	den	einem	einer	einem	keinen

Ich gebe **dem Elektriker** einen Scheck.
I give the electrician a cheque. / I give a cheque to the electrician.

Ich zeige **einem Kunden** das Buch.
I show a customer the book ./ I show the book to a customer.

C In the dative case, the noun adds an -(e)n in the plural, unless it already ends in -n or -s.

Ich bringe **den Kindern**   *I'll bring the children a*
ein Geschenk.   *present.*

D The following verbs are always followed by the dative case: bringen *to bring*; erzählen *to tell*; geben *to give*; sagen *to say*; schicken *to send*; zeigen *to show*; antworten* *to answer*; danken* *to thank*; folgen* *to follow*; helfen* *to help*.

*These verbs do not have an indirect object in English.

Paul gibt **dem Mädchen** ein   *Paul gives the girl a present. /*
Geschenk.   *Paul gives a present to the*
                                   girl.
Der Manager dankt **der Frau.**   *The manager thanks the*
                                   woman.

exercise

1 Complete the sentences with the dative case. The gender of the noun is given in brackets to help you. Don't forget to add the dative plural ending where necessary.

E.g. Ich schicke _____ Frau (*f.*) eine Karte. →
Ich schicke *der* Frau eine Karte.

a Herr Bühler gibt _____ Chef (*m.*) den Brief.
b Mutti bringt _____ Kind (*nt.*) ein Spielzeug.
c Der Polizist hilft _____ Autofahrer (*m.*)
d Ich sage _____ Lehrerin (*f.*) nichts.
e Er zeigt _____ Mädchen (*nt.*) ein Foto.
f Ich erzähle_____ Kinder_____ (*pl.*) eine Geschichte.

The genitive case indicates possession in German. In English, we express this with of or use an apostrophe.

A Here is a summary of the article in the genitive case.

	m.	f.	nt.	pl.	m.	f.	nt.	pl.
nom.	der	die	das	die	ein	eine	ein	keine
gen.	des	der	des	der	eines	einer	eines	keiner

Der Manager **der** Firma heißt   *The manager of the firm /*
Herr Frank.   *The firm's manager is*
                                   called Mr Frank.

In the masculine and neuter forms -s, or -es (with nouns of one syllable) is added to most nouns.

die Bluse **des** Mädchens   *the girl's blouse*
Sie ist die Schwester **eines** Freundes. *She is the sister of a friend.*

B With names of people, nationalities, towns and cities, you can make a possessive form by adding an -s to the name.

Annettes Buch   *Annette's book*
Deutschlands Hauptstadt   *Germany's capital (city)*

C Certain expressions take the genitive case:

Anfang **des Monats** (*m.*) fahre ich   *I'm going to Stuttgart at*
nach Stuttgart.   *the beginning of the*
                                        month.

Ende **der Woche** (*f.*)/**des Jahres** (*nt.*) *at the end of the week/the*
                                        year

D The genitive case is generally used in written German but less often in spoken German. In everyday conversation, **von** + the dative case is often used instead of the genitive.

der Bruder **des Mannes** (gen.) (m.)   *the man's brother*
der Bruder von dem Mann (dat.) (m.) *the brother of the man*

exercises

1 Make sentences and add the genitive -s ending to the names.

a England_____	Hafen	höre ich gern.
b Frankreich_____	Musik	heißt Elizabeth.
c Hamburg_____	Hauptstadt	trinke ich gern.
d Italien_____	Filme	sehe ich gern.
e Steven Spielberg_____	Weine	ist Rom.
f Beethoven_____	Königin	ist an der Elbe.

2 Complete these sentences with the correct form of the genitive and add an ending to the noun where necessary.

E.g. Ende _____ Woche (f.) gehe ich in Urlaub. →
Ende *der* Woche gehe ich in Urlaub.

a Das Büro _____ Chef_____ (m.) ist im ersten Stock.
b Das Haus _____ Familie (f.) Schmidt ist groß.
c Anfang _____ Jahr_____ (nt.) fahre ich nach Paris.
d Die Jacke _____ Frau (f.) ist sehr modisch.
e Mitte _____ Monat_____ (m.) fliegen wir nach Spanien.
f Der Elektriker _____ Firma (f.) Hansen arbeitet samstags.

Dieser (this), jeder (every), etc. (called determiners) take similar endings to der, die, das. Like der, die and das, they are usually used with nouns.

Dieser Zug fährt nach Köln. *This train is going to Cologne.*

A The most common determiners are: **dieser** *this, these,* **mancher** *many,* **jeder** *each, every,* **jener** *that* and **welcher?** *which?*

B Dies-, manch-, jed-, jen-, welch- add similar endings to **der**, **die** and **das**. The following table shows the nominative endings.

m.	f.	nt.	pl.
der	die	das	die
dieser	diese	dieses	diese
jeder	jede	jedes	– (*no plural*)
jener	jene	jenes	jene
mancher	manche	manches	manche
welcher	welche	welches	welche

Dieser Wein (*m.*) schmeckt gut. *This wine tastes good.*
Jener Wein (*m.*) schmeckt besser. *That wine tastes better.*
Jedes Haus (*nt.*) hat einen Garten. *Every house has a garden.*
Manche Leute (*pl.*) sind reich. *Many people are rich.*
Welche Farbe (*f.*)? *What colour?*

C Dieser etc. take similar case endings to der, die and das in the other cases.

	m.	f.	nt.	pl.
nom.	dieser	diese	dieses	diese
acc.	diesen	diese	dieses	diese
dat.	diesem	dieser	diesem	diesen
gen.	dieses	dieser	dieses	dieser

Ich möchte **diesen Pullover** (*m. acc.*) kaufen.	*I'd like to buy this pullover.*
Ich fahre **jede Woche** (*f. acc.*) in die Stadt.	*I go to town every week.*
Er war **dieses Jahr** (*nt. acc.*) in Barcelona.	*He was in Barcelona this year.*

exercise

1 Add the correct endings to dies-, etc. Use the nominative case.

E.g. Welch_____ Buch (*nt.*) ist das? → Welch**es** Buch ist das?

a Dies_____ Kleid (*nt.*) war sehr teuer.

b Welch_____ Film (*m.*) läuft im Kino?

c Jed_____ Kind (*nt.*) liebt Schokolade.

d Manch_____ Leute (*pl.*) fahren gern nach Italien.

e Welch_____ Tag (*m.*) ist heute?

f Dies_____ Woche (*f.*) ist eine Ausstellung in der Stadt.

g Welch_____ Zug (*m.*) fährt nach München?

Mein (my), sein (his), etc. are used before a noun to show possession.

Das ist **meine** Schwester. *That's my sister.*

A The possessives:

mein	my	**unser**	our
dein	your (familiar, singular)	**euer**	your (familiar, plural)
sein	his, its	**ihr**	their
ihr	her		
Ihr	your (formal, singular and plural)		

B Possessive endings are the same as for **ein, eine, ein,** etc.

	m.	f.	nt.	pl.
nom.	mein	meine	mein	meine
acc.	meinen	meine	mein	meine
dat.	meinem	meiner	meinem	meinen
gen.	meines	meiner	meines	meiner

Mein Name (*f. nom.*) ist Tina.   *My name is Tina.*

Wir besuchen **unseren Onkel** (*m. acc.*).   *We are visiting our uncle.*

Kennst du **seine Schwester** (*f. acc.*)?   *Do you know his sister?*

Ich helfe **meiner Mutter** (*f. dat.*).

I'm helping my mother.

Die Frau **deines Bruders** (*m. gen.*) ist in Braunschweig.

Your brother's wife is in Braunschweig.

exercises

1 Add an ending to the possessive where necessary. Use the nominative case.

E.g. mein_____ Onkel → mein Onkel

    sein_____ Tante → seine Tante

a mein_____ Vater

b sein_____ Mutter

c ihr_____ Schwester

d unser_____ Bruder

e dein_____ Großmutter

f euer_____ Großvater

g mein_____ Tante

h Ihr_____ Onkel

2 Complete the sentences with the correct possessive pronoun.

a Manfred ist Katis Freund. Manfred ist _____ Freund.

b Sabine ist Karles Frau. Sabine ist _____ Frau.

c Regina ist Tanjas Tante. Tanja ist _____ Nichte.

d Frank ist Pauls Vater. Frank ist _____ Vater.

e Ich habe einen Bruder. Er heißt Uwe. Uwe ist _____ Bruder.

Some masculine nouns (der words) often take an -n or -en ending. They are known as weak nouns.

A Weak masculine nouns add an -n or -en ending in all cases except the nominative singular. The endings are added after **der, dieser, ein, mein**, etc. Look at the following table for **der Junge** (*the boy*).

	singular	plural
nom.	**der** Junge	**die** Jungen
acc.	**den** Jungen	**die** Jungen
dat.	**dem** Jungen	**den** Jungen
gen.	**des** Jungen	**der** Jungen

Der Kunde ist im Büro.
Ich treffe **den** Kunden am Freitag.

The customer is in the office.
I'm meeting the customer on Friday.

B Other weak masculine nouns

- male persons and creatures ending in -e: der Affe *monkey*; der Kollege *colleague*; der Kunde *customer*; der Neffe *nephew*; der Brite *Briton*.
- male persons ending in -t: der Architekt *architect*; der Demokrat *democrat*; der Polizist *policeman*; der Präsident *president*.

- masculine nouns ending in: **-ant**, **-nom** and **-og(e)**: der Elefant *elephant*; der Astronom *astronomer*; der Psychologe *psychologist*.

C Most weak nouns add **-n**: der Bauer *farmer*; der Nachbar *neighbour*.

However, some add **-en** ...: der Katholik *Catholic*; der Mensch *human being*.

... and others add **-n** in the singular and **-en** in the plural: der Herr *gentleman, Mr.*

exercise

1 Say whether the following weak nouns take an **-n** or an **-en** ending.

a der Mensch
b der Junge
c der Bauer
d der Präsident
e der Kollege
f der Nachbar
g der Architekt
h der Demokrat
i der Neffe
j der Katholik

A verb describes an action or a state. The tense, for example present, past, etc., expresses when this action takes place.

Die Kinder **spielen**. *The children are playing.*

A When you look up a verb in the dictionary, you will find the infinitive form. In German, most infinitives end in **-en**. A few end only in **-n**: spiel**en** *to play*; kauf**en** *to buy*; sei**n** *to be*.

B In German, there is only one form of the present tense which can translate both English forms.

Ich spiele Golf. *I play golf./I am playing golf.*

C The verb stem is the part of the infinitive without <u>-en</u>.

spielen → spiel   kaufen → kauf

D In the present tense, the following endings are added to the verb stem.

spielen	to play		
ich spiele	I play	wir spielen	we play
du spielst	you (sing.) play	ihr spielt	you (pl.) play
er/sie/es spielt	he/she/it plays	sie spielen	they play
		Sie spielen	you (polite sing. and pl.) play

Ich besuche meine Freundin. *I visit my (girl)friend.*
Was **machst du**? *What are you doing?*
Jan kauft einen Comic. *Jan buys a comic.*
Karin bleibt zu Hause. *Karin is staying at home.*
Wir kommen um sieben Uhr. *We're coming at seven o'clock.*
Geht ihr ins Kino? *Are you going to the cinema?*
Sie wohnen in Freiburg. *They live in Freiburg.*

exercise

1 Fill in the other half of the dominoes with a verb from the box to make matching pairs. There is often more than one possible answer.

telefoniert	macht	kommt	geht	studieren	wohnst
	kaufen	besuchen	spiele		

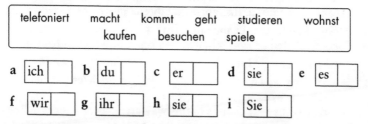

a ich ☐   b du ☐   c er ☐   d sie ☐   e es ☐

f wir ☐   g ihr ☐   h sie ☐   i Sie ☐

In the present tense, some verbs do not follow the regular pattern. They change their stem or spelling in certain parts of the verb.

A Verbs which end in -den, -ten or -nen add an extra **e** before the verb ending in the **du**, **er/sie/es** and **ihr** forms: **arbeiten** *to work*, **finden** *to find*, **kosten** *to cost*, **warten** *to wait*, **regnen** *to rain*.

> arbeiten → du arbeitest, er/sie/es arbeitet, ihr arbeitet
> Es regnet.   *It's raining.*

B Verbs which end in -sen, -ßen, -ssen or -zen add -t (not -st) in the **du** form: **reisen** *to travel*, **hassen** *to hate*, **heißen** *to be called*, **tanzen** *to dance*.

> reisen → du reist
> Wie heißt du?   *What are you called?*

C In German, an important group of verbs are known as *strong verbs*. In the present tense, the vowel (**a**, **e**) in the middle changes in the **du** and **er/sie/es** forms of most strong verbs.

- a → ä, e.g. **fahren** *to go, travel*: ich fahre, du fährst, er/sie/es fährt, wir fahren, ihr fahrt, sie fahren, Sie fahren

  Other verbs that change in this way are **tragen** *to wear, carry*, **laufen** *to run*, **schlafen** *to sleep* and **waschen** *to wash*.

  Er trägt einen Hut.   *He's wearing a hat.*

- e → i, e.g. **essen** *to eat*: ich esse, du isst, er/sie/es isst, wir essen, ihr esst, sie essen, Sie essen

  Other verbs that change in this way are: **geben** *to give*, **helfen** *to help*, **nehmen** *to take*, **sprechen** *to speak*, **treffen** *to meet*.

- e → ie, e.g. **lesen** *to read*: ich lese, **du liest**, **er/sie/es liest**, wir lesen, ihr lest, sie lesen, Sie lesen; **sehen** *to see* ich sehe, **du siehst**, **er/sie/es** sieht, wir sehen, ihr sehst, sie sehen, Sie sehen

exercises

1 **Complete the sentences. Use the present tense of one of the verbs from the box.**

| tragen fahren sprechen waschen lesen schlafen geben |

E.g. Ich _____ gern Bücher. → Ich lese gern Bücher.

a Herr Hofmeister _____ Englisch und Deutsch.

b Samstags _____ die Kinder bis zehn Uhr.

c Karola _____ die Socken.

d Er _____ Tobias zehn Mark.

e Ihr _____ schwarze Jeans.

f Der Bus _____ in die Stadt.

2 **Make sentences to say what they are doing.**

E.g. Sebastian/im Wald/laufen → Sebastian läuft im Wald.

a Kerstin/nach Paris/fahren

b Frau Link/am Computer/arbeiten

c Monika/im Restaurant/essen

d Du/nächste Woche/nach London/reisen

e Andreas/Apfelstrudel mit Sahne/essen

f Du/einen blauen Pullover/tragen

g Peter/Zeitung/lesen

Some verbs follow a different pattern to most other verbs. They are called irregular verbs.

A Two very important irregular verbs are **haben** *to have* and **sein** *to be*. They are irregular in both English and German.

haben	to have		
ich habe	*I have*	wir haben	*we have*
du hast	*you have*	ihr habt	*you have*
er/sie/es hat	*he/she/it has*	sie haben	*they have*
		Sie haben	*you have*

sein	to be		
ich bin	*I am*	wir sind	*we are*
du bist	*you are*	ihr seid	*you are*
er/sie/es ist	*he/she/it is*	sie sind	*they are*
		Sie sind	*you are*

Er hat einen Hund.	*He has a dog.*
Wir haben eine neue Wohnung.	*We have a new flat.*
Sie ist Ärztin.	*She is a doctor.*
Wie alt **bist du**?	*How old are you?*
Ich bin zwanzig Jahre alt.	*I am twenty years old.*

The verb **haben** (not **sein**!) is used in these phrases.

Ich habe Durst.	*I am thirsty.*
Er hat Hunger.	*He's hungry.*
Wir haben Angst.	*We are frightened.*

Sie hat Glück.   *She is lucky.*

Ich habe keine Lust.   *I don't want to.*

exercises

1 Complete each sentence with a verb from the list.

ist	habe	sind	hast	~~haben~~	bist	ist
	hat	sind	seid	hat		

E.g. Wir _____ ein großes Haus. → Wir haben ein großes Haus.

a Das Haus _____ einen Garten.   h Ich _____ Hunger.

b Johann _____ bei einer Bank.   i Du _____ mein bester

c Die Kinder _____ Zwillinge.   Freund.

d Er _____ 30 Jahre alt.   j Wo _____ wir?

e _____ ihr heute zu Hause?

f Frau Kraft _____ eine Schwester.

g _____ du heute Abend Zeit?

2 Complete the sentences with haben or sein.

E.g. Ich _____ einen Bruder und zwei Schwestern. →
Ich habe einen Bruder und zwei Schwestern.

a Daniel _____ Mechaniker.

b Wir _____ Engländerinnen.

c Nina _____ blondes Haar und blaue Augen.

d Ich _____ keine Lust.

e _____ du Geschwister?

f Maria _____ Angst vor dem Hund.

g Sie (*they*) _____ einen Termin beim Arzt.

The imperative or command form is used to tell people what to do and to make requests and suggestions.

A There are three words for *you* in German: **du** (singular, familiar); **ihr** (plural, familiar); and **Sie** (singular and plural, polite).

Du bist mein Bruder.	*You are my brother.*
Ihr seid meine Brüder.	*You are my brothers.*
Sind Sie Arzt?	*Are you a doctor?*

B As there are three words for *you* in German, there are three imperative forms. There is often an exclamation mark after the command form.

- **du**: use the present-tense **du** form without **-st** and without **du**. If there is an umlaut, leave it off.
  du kommst → **Komm!** *Come!*
  du isst → **Iss!** *Eat!*
  du fährst → **Fahr!** *Go!*

- **ihr**: use the present-tense **ihr** form but leave out **ihr**.
  ihr steht → **Steht!**

- **Sie**: use the present-tense **Sie** form but put **Sie** after the verb.
  Sie gehen → **Gehen Sie!**

C The verb **sein** has an irregular imperative form.

du → **Sei ruhig!**
ihr → **Seid ruhig!**   } *Be quiet!*
Sie → **Seien Sie ruhig!**

D With separable verbs, the separable part (prefix) goes to the end of the sentence:

mitkommen → **Komm** mal **mit!** *Come with us!*

E The infinitive is often used instead of the imperative in instructions, e.g. in recipes and on signs.

Mehl und Zucker **mischen.**   *Mix the flour and the sugar.*
Bitte nicht **stören.**   *Please do not disturb.*

exercise

1 Complete these sentences with the familiar imperative form of the verb in brackets.

E.g. Anna, _____ dir das Bild an! (sehen) →
Anna, *sieh* dir das Bild an!

a Alex, _____ bitte ruhig! (sein)
b Sandra, _____ bitte den Text vor! (lesen)
c _____ ihr bitte die Suppe! (essen)
d Simone, _____ jetzt! (schlafen)
e Ludwig, _____ bitte langsamer! (fahren)

The perfect tense is a past tense used mostly in spoken German for describing events that have already happened.

Er **hat** gestern Golf **gespielt**. *He played golf yesterday.*

A The perfect tense of most verbs is formed with the present tense of the verb **haben** and the past participle. The perfect tense in German is often used for the present perfect tense as well as the simple past tense in English.

Wir **haben getanzt**.   *We have danced/We danced.*

B The past participle is formed from the infinitive. Take off the -en ending to leave the stem. Add **ge-** to the front of the stem and -t to the end. Verbs that have a regular stem and form their past participles with a -t ending are known as *weak verbs*.

tanzen → **ge**tanz**t** *danced*   hören → **ge**hör**t** (*heard*)

C The perfect tense of the verb **kaufen** *to buy*:

ich habe gekauft	wir haben gekauft
du hast gekauft	ihr habt gekauft
er/sie/es hat gekauft	sie haben gekauft
	Sie haben gekauft

D Note the word order when using the perfect tense. The form of **haben** is the second idea in the sentence. The past participle goes to the end.

Wir haben Musik **gehört**.	*We listened/have listened to music.*
Ich habe letzten Montag Fitnesstraining **gemacht**.	*I did fitness training last Monday.*
Gestern **habe ich** Tennis **gespielt**.	*I played tennis yesterday.*

exercises

1 Match each subject to the correct perfect tense verb.

a	du	1	haben gefragt
b	ich	2	habt gesagt
c	wir	3	hast geduscht
d	er	4	habe getanzt
e	ihr	5	hat gekauft

2 Complete the sentences with the perfect tense of the verb.

E.g. Ich _____ eine Jacke _____ . (kaufen) →

Ich *habe* eine Jacke *gekauft*.

a Er _____ das Mittagessen _____ . (kochen)
b Wir _____ das Wohnzimmer _____ . (putzen)
c Silvia _____ zehn Jahre in Frankfurt _____ . (wohnen)
d Sie (*they*) _____ am Wochenende nichts _____ . (machen)

A group of verbs known as strong verbs have past participles with an -en ending.

Ich **habe** gestern die Zeitung **gelesen.**   *I read the newspaper yesterday.*

A Most strong verbs form the past participle by adding **ge-** to the front of the infinitive. The past participle, like the infinitive, ends in **-en.**

geben → **gegeben** *gave*   lesen → **gelesen** *read*
sehen → **gesehen** *saw*   essen → **gegessen** *eaten*

Wir **haben** Franz **gesehen.**   *We saw/have seen Franz.*

B Other past participles have a vowel change in the middle.

• **ei → ie**, e.g. schreiben → **geschrieben** *written*
• **e → o** , e.g. helfen → **geholfen** *helped*
  nehmen → **genommen** *taken*   treffen → **getroffen** *met*
• **i → u**, e.g. finden → **gefunden** *found*
  trinken → **getrunken** *drunk*   singen → **gesungen** *sung*

Stefan **hat** einen Brief **geschrieben.**   *Stefan wrote/has written a letter.*

Heike **hat** Ruth **getroffen.**   *Heike met/has met Ruth.*
Wir **haben** gestern Abend   *We drank red wine*
  Rotwein **getrunken.**   *yesterday evening.*

exercises

1 Complete each sentence with the past participle of the verb in brackets.

E.g. Gestern habe ich ein Buch _____ . (lesen) →
      Gestern habe ich ein Buch **gelesen**.

a Alex hat vier Postkarten aus Italien _____ . (schreiben)
b Daniela war krank. Sie hat eine Tablette _____ . (nehmen)
c Ich habe meiner Mutter Blumen _____ . (geben)
d Habt ihr den neuen James Bond Film _____ ? (sehen)
e Am Sonntag haben wir im Restaurant _____ . (essen)

2 Complete the verb table with the help of the verb list in Unit 88.

	verb	past participle	meaning
E.g.	bitten	gebeten	*to ask, to request*
a	fangen		
b		geschlafen	
c			*to cut*
d	schließen		
e	tun		
f			*to leave, to let*

Some verbs in the perfect tense form the past participle in an irregular way.

Es **hat** am Montag **geregnet**.
It rained on Monday.

A Weak verbs ending in **-ten**, **-den** or **-nen** add an extra **-e** before the **-t** ending (to make them easier to pronounce):

warten → gewartet *waited*   reden → geredet *talked*
kosten → gekostet *cost*   antworten → geantwortet
regnen → geregnet *rained*   *answered*

Ich **habe** vor dem Kino **gewartet**. *I waited in front of the cinema.*

B Weak verbs ending in **-ieren** add **-t** to the end of the stem but no **ge-** at the front:

telefonieren → **telefoniert** *telephoned*   studieren → **studiert** *studied*

David **hat** mit Susanna **telefoniert**. *David (has) phoned Susanna.*

C The past participle of the irregular verb **haben** is **gehabt**.

Renate **hat** einen Unfall **gehabt**. *Renate (has) had an accident.*

D Some verbs are known as mixed verbs because they form the past participle with a -t ending like weak verbs but have a vowel change in the middle like strong verbs.

bringen → **gebracht** *brought*   denken → **gedacht** (*thought*)
kennen → **gekannt** *known* (*a person*)
wissen → **gewusst** *known* (*a fact*)

Ich **habe** das nicht **gewusst**.   *I didn't know that.*

exercises

1 Fill in the missing letters in the past participles.
E.g. Ich habe s_ud_er_ . → Ich habe studiert.

a Du hast es _ewu_ _t.
b Ihr habt s_ud_ _r_.
c Sie haben ein Eis _eh_ _t.
d Ich habe Bjorn g_k_nn_.

2 Write sentences in the perfect tense.
E.g. Das T-Shirt /25 Euro/kosten →
Das T-Shirt hat 25 Euro gekostet.

a Wir/eine Stunde/warten
b Ich/im Büro/arbeiten
c Es/den ganzen Tag/regnen
d Beate/mit Markus/telefonieren
e Wir/Glück/haben
f Georg/in Berlin/studieren
g Ich/ihm/antworten

Some verbs form the perfect tense with the present tense of the verb sein and a past participle.

A Look at the perfect tense of **fliegen** *to fly*, which uses **sein**.

ich bin geflogen	wir sind geflogen
du bist geflogen	ihr seid geflogen
er/sie/es ist geflogen	sie sind geflogen
	Sie sind geflogen

Wir **sind** nach Spanien **geflogen**. *We flew to Spain.*

B Most verbs used with **sein** in the perfect tense are verbs of movement. Here are some useful past participles. Most of them take an **-en** ending (strong verbs) but a few take a **-t** ending (weak verbs).

verb	past participle	meaning
fahren	gefahren	*driven*
fallen	gefallen	*fallen*
fliegen	geflogen	*flown*
gehen	gegangen	*gone*
kommen	gekommen	*come*
laufen	gelaufen	*run*
reiten	geritten	*ridden*
schwimmen	geschwommen	*swum*
steigen	gestiegen	*climbed*

reisen	gereist	*travelled*
segeln	gesegelt	*sailed*
wandern	gewandert	*hiked*

Sebastian **ist** um 23 Uhr gekommen.

Sebastian arrived at 11 p.m.

Ich **bin** gestern **gewandert**.

I went hiking yesterday.

exercise

1 Last summer you went on holiday to Spain. Complete the postcard.

a fliegen   c fahren   e reiten
b gehen   d schwimmen   f segeln

Liebe Julia,

wir **a** *sind* nach Spanien *geflogen*. Am Sonntag **b** _____ wir zum Strand _____ . Am nächsten Tag **c** _____ wir in die Berge _____ . Am Mittwoch **d** _____ ich im Meer _____ . Klaus und ich **e** _____ am Strand _____ . Am letzten Tag _____ wir **f** _____ . Das war toll!

Deine Claudia

Some other verbs also use sein in the perfect tense. Some verbs can use both haben and sein.

A Useful verbs with **sein** in the perfect tense.

verb	past participle	meaning
bleiben	geblieben	*stayed*
sein	geworden	*been*
sinken	gesunken	*sunk*
sterben	gestorben	*died*
werden	geworden	*become*
passieren	passiert	*happened*
verschwinden	verschwunden	*disappeared*
gebären	geboren	*born*
gesschehen	geschehen	*happened*

Was **ist** gestern **passiert**? *What happened yesterday?*

Verbs which have a **ge-** prefix do not add a second **ge-**.

Das Baby **ist** am 25. August **geboren**. *The baby was born on 25th August.*

B A few verbs which can use either **haben** or **sein** in the perfect tense.

fahren	gefahren	*driven*
reiten	geritten	*ridden*
schwimmen	geschwommen	*swum*
segeln	gesegelt	*sailed*

These verbs use **haben** in the perfect tense when they have a
direct object; if there isn't a direct object, they use **sein**.

Ich **bin** nach München **gefahren**. *I drove to Munich.*
Ich **habe** *das Auto* nach München *I drove **the car** to Munich.*
  gefahren.

exercises

1 Fill in the missing letters in these past participles. Then
write down the infinitive together with its English meaning.
E.g. g_f_hr_n → gefahren; fahren (*to go*)

a _es_hwo_me_   c g_w_r_en
b ge_it _ _n   d _ew_s_ _

2 Complete the sentences with the perfect tense.

E.g. Ich _____ Arzt _____ . (werden) → Ich bin Arzt geworden.
a Meine Oma _____ 1925 _____ .   (gebären)
b Sie _____ vor drei Jahren _____ .   (sterben)
c Ich _____ zu Hause _____ .   (bleiben)
d Sie schon in Deutschland _____ ?   (sein)
e Herzlichen Glückwunsch! Du _____ Vater _____ .
                                         (werden)

There is another past tense in German which is known as the simple past or imperfect tense.

Gestern **besuchte** der Premierminister Deutschland.

Yesterday the prime minister visted Germany.

A In the simple past, endings are added to the stem of weak verbs. The stem is the infinitive without -en. Look at the simple past of **spielen** (*to play*).

ich spiel**te**	wir spiel**ten**
du spiel**test**	ihr spiel**tet**
er/sie/es spiel**te**	sie spiel**ten**
	Sie spiel**ten**

Ich spielte Tennis.   *I played tennis.*

B Verbs ending in -den, -ten, -nen add an extra -e- before the endings to make them easier to pronounce:

reden → **ich** red**ete** *I talked*   warten → **wir** wart**eten** (*we waited*)

regnen → **es** regn**ete** *it rained*

Er **wartete** eine Stunde.   *He waited for an hour.*

C The simple past is mainly used in written German (newspapers, books) to describe past events, whereas the perfect tense is used more often in spoken German.

• The simple past describes finished actions in written German.

Jens Lang **arbeitete** in einer Fabrik. *Jens Lang worked in a factory.*

- It expresses the English past continuous form in written and spoken German.
  Während ich Musik **hörte**, **telefonierte** Silke.
  While I was listening to music, Silke was telephoning.

- It can express the English *used to*.
  Früher **wohnten** wir in Heidelberg.
  We used to live in Heidelberg.

exercises

1 Make six sentences from the table.
E.g. Es regnete den ganzen Tag.

Es	spielte	in dem Büro.
Sie	hörtest	**den ganzen Tag.**
Wir	arbeiteten	in München.
Ich	**regnete**	zehn Minuten.
Sie (*she*)	wohnten	mit seiner Frau.
Er	wartete	Musik.
Du	telefonierte	Tennis.

2 Make sentences to say what they bought.
E.g. ich/eine Jeanshose → Ich kaufte eine Jeanshose.

a du/ein Auto
b er/eine Jacke
c sie (*they*)/ein Buch
d wir/Bananen
e Sie/einen Fernseher
f ihr/Äpfel
g sie (*she*)/eine Bluse

Some verbs are used in the simple past form in both spoken and written German.

Sie **fuhren** mit dem Bus in die Stadt.
They went to town by bus.

A In the simple past, strong verbs change in the main part of the verb. The endings are added to the new stem.

Look at **gehen** *to go* which has the simple past stem **ging**.

ich ging	wir gingen
du gingst	ihr gingt
er/sie/es ist **ging**	sie gingen
	Sie gingen

B The following strong verbs are used not only in written German but are also frequently used in conversation.

verb	simple past stem	meaning
bleiben	blieb	*stayed*
essen	aß	*ate*
fahren	fuhr	*went, drove*
finden	fand	*found*
geben	gab	*gave*
kommen	kam	*came*

lesen	las	*read*
schwimmen	**schwamm**	*swam*
sehen	**sah**	*saw*
treffen	**traf**	*met*

exercises

1 Find six verbs in the simple past in the word square. Then match each verb to a suitable personal pronoun.

E.g. er sah
a ihr
b wir
c es
d du
e Sie

E	G	A	B	T	G	M	P
L	A	S	E	N	I	N	S
R	K	A	M	E	N	Ü	I
I	S	H	O	D	G	H	A
F	N	F	U	H	R	S	T

2 Complete the story with the correct form of the simple past from the box. You will need to use one verb more than once.

| blieben | gingen | kam | gab | ging | traf |

Ich **a** _____ gestern in die Stadt. Im Kaufhaus **b** _____ ich meine Freunde und wir **c** _____ ins Cafe. Es **d** _____ Kaffee und Kuchen. Danach **e** _____ wir ins Kino. Es **f** _____ ein James Bond Film. Dann **g** _____ wir bis 1.00 Uhr in der Kneipe.

The irregular verbs haben, sein and werden have irregular forms in the simple past. Mixed verbs also follow a different pattern.

A The simple past form of **haben** and **sein** is used in written and spoken German much more frequently than the perfect tense. **Haben** has an irregular stem and takes weak verb endings, whereas **sein** has an irregular stem and adds strong verb endings.

haben *to have*	
ich hatte	wir hatten
du hattest	ihr hattet
er/sie/es hatte	sie hatten
	Sie hatten

Ich **hatte** zwei Wochen Urlaub.   *I had two weeks' holiday.*

sein *to be*	
ich war	wir waren
du warst	ihr wart
er/sie/es war	sie waren
	Sie waren

Im Sommer **war** er in Italien.   *He was in Italy in the summer.*

Mixed verbs have an irregular verb stem. They take weak verb endings.

bringen → **ich brachte** *I brought*
denken → **ich dachte** *I thought*
kennen → **ich kannte** *I knew (a person)*
wissen → **ich wusste** *I knew (a fact)*

Ich **wusste**, dass es spät war.   *I knew it was late.*

The verb **werden** *to become* also has an irregular stem (**wurde**) and takes strong verb endings.

Ich **wurde** müde.   *I became tired.*

The separable prefix of separable verbs goes to the end of the sentence.

anfangen *to start*:
Das Konzert **fing** um 20 Uhr **an**. *The concert started at 8 pm.*

exercise

1 Complete the sentences with the correct form of haben or sein.

E.g. Ich _____ keine Zeit. → Ich hatte keine Zeit.
a Er _____ vorgestern Kopfschmerzen.
b Gestern Nachmittag _____ ich in der Stadt.
c Wir _____ einen Unfall auf der Autobahn.
d Sie (*She*) _____ Glück.
e Ich _____ letzte Woche krank.
f Wo _____ du am Samstag?
g Ich _____ eine Woche Urlaub.

There are six modal verbs in German. Used to make requests, ask permission, etc., they are often used with another verb.

A The modal verbs in German are:

dürfen *to be allowed to*	**müssen** *to have to*
können *to be able to*	**sollen** *to be supposed to*
mögen *to like*	**wollen** *to want to*

B

dürfen *to be allowed to, may*	
ich darf	wir dürfen
du darfst	ihr dürft
er/sie/es/man darf	sie dürfen
	Sie dürfen

Ich **darf** nicht **rauchen**.   *I'm not allowed to smoke.*

Man (*one*) takes the **er/sie/es** form of the verb, and is often used to say what one can/may/must (not) do.

Man darf hier (nicht) **parken**.   *One is (not) allowed to park here.*

C

können *to be able to, can*	
ich kann	wir können
du kannst	ihr könnt
er/sie/es kann	sie können
	Sie können

Ich **kann** Deutsch **sprechen**.   *I can speak German.*
Wir **können** das Theater   *We can visit the theatre.*
  besuchen.

D Modal verbs are normally used with another verb in the infinitive. This verb goes to the end of the sentence.
    Er **kann** gut **schwimmen**.   *He can swim well.*

exercises

1 What is one not allowed to do here?

E.g. rauchen → **Man darf hier nicht rauchen.**

a parken
b baden
c fotografieren
d essen

2 What can these people do at the weekend?

E.g. Wir/ins Konzert → **Wir können ins Konzert gehen.**

a ihr/ins Kino
b wir/zum Fußball
c sie (*they*)/zum Weinfest
d du/ins Theater
e Renate/ins Jazzhaus
f Lorenz/zum Schwimmbad

Mögen (to like), müssen (to have to), sollen (to be supposed to) and wollen (to want to) are the other four modal verbs in German.

A | mögen *to like*

ich mag	wir mögen
du magst	ihr mögt
er/sie/es mag	sie mögen
	Sie mögen

Er **mag** Golf **spielen**.   *He likes playing golf.*

Mögen is often used with a noun.

Ich **mag** Tee.   *I like tea.*

B | müssen *to have to, must*

ich muss	wir müssen
du musst	ihr müsst
er/sie/es muss	sie müssen
	Sie müssen

Ich **muss** zur Arbeit **gehen**.   *I must go to work.*

müssen + nicht = needn't

Ich **muss** morgen **nicht arbeiten**.   *I don't have to/needn't work tomorrow.*

C | **sollen** *to be supposed to, should*

ich soll	wir sollen
du sollst	ihr sollt
er/sie/es soll	sie sollen
	Sie sollen

Ich **soll** zum Arzt **gehen**. *I should go to the doctor's.*
Du **sollst** eine Fahrkarte **kaufen**. *You should buy a ticket.*

D | **wollen** *to want to*

ich will	wir wollen
du willst	ihr wollt
er/sie/es will	sie wollen
	Sie wollen

Er **will** seine Oma **besuchen**. *He wants to visit his*
grandma.

exercise

1 Add the correct form of the verbs.

E.g. Wir _____ zum Zahnarzt _____ . (sollen/gehen) →
Wir sollen zum Zahnarzt gehen.

a Er _____ samstags _____ . (müssen/arbeiten)
b _____ du Karten _____ ? (wollen/spielen)
c Ich _____ Krimis. (mögen)
d Alexander _____ uns im Garten _____ . (sollen/helfen)
e Die Kinder _____ nicht _____ . (müssen/warten)

The verb lassen has several meanings in German.

A Ich **lasse** mir die Haare **schneiden**. *I am having my hair cut.*

lassen (present tense)	
ich lasse	wir lassen
du lässt	ihr lässt
er/sie/es lässt	sie lassen
	Sie lassen

B **Lassen** can mean *to have something done*. You use the appropriate tense (present, past) of the verb **lassen** + the infinitive form of the second verb. The infinitive goes to the end of the sentence. (In English, the second verb is a past participle.)

Ich **lasse** das Auto **reparieren**.   *I'm having the car repaired*

C In German, the dative personal pronouns are used when referring to parts of the body.

Ich **lasse** mir die Haare **schneiden**. *I'm having my hair cut.*

D **Lassen** can also mean:

• *to leave*
  Ich **lasse** meine Jacke hier.   *I'll leave my jacket here.*

• *to let, allow*
  Ich **lasse** die Kinder am Computer *I let the children play on*
    spielen.   *the computer.*

Lass mich sehen.   *Let me have a look.*

- *to stop*

  lass (du), **lassen Sie (Sie)** and **lasst (ihr)** are the three
  command forms.

  Lass das! ⎫
  Lasst das! ⎬   *Stop that!*
  Lassen Sie das! ⎭

exercises

1 **Add the correct form of lassen + infinitive.**

E.g. wir/das Auto reparieren → Wir lassen das Auto reparieren.

a ich/die Fenster putzen   e ich/die Uhr reparieren
b er/den Film entwickeln   f du/die Schuhe reparieren
c ich/meine Augen untersuchen   g ich/mir die Haare schneiden
d Frau Schmidt/das Zimmer streichen

2 **Choose the correct form of lassen for each sentence.**

lassen	lass	lässt	lass	lasse	lass

a _____ das!
b Andrea _____ den Hund zu Hause.
c _____ Tobias dein Buch lesen!
d Ich _____ das Geld auf dem Tisch.
e Wir _____ den Fernseher reparieren.
f _____ mich das machen!

The simple past forms of the modal verbs are often used instead of the perfect tense forms in German.

A dürfen → ich durfte *I was allowed to*
können → ich konnte *I was able to, I could*
mögen → ich mochte *I liked*
müssen → ich musste *I had to*
sollen → ich sollte *I was supposed to*
wollen → ich wollte *I wanted to*

B To form the simple past, the following endings are added to the verb stem.

ich	-te	wir	-ten
du	-test	ihr	-tet
er/sie/es	-te	sie	-ten
		Sie	-ten

C If the vowel of the stem has an umlaut, the umlaut is dropped.

können → ich konnte   müssen → wir mussten
mögen → er mochte

können *to be able to*	
ich konnte	wir konnten
du konntest	ihr konntet
er/sie/es konnte	sie konnten
	Sie konnten

Ich **konnte** mit sechzehn   *I was able to ride a*
Motorrad fahren.   *motorbike at sixteen.*

D Modal verbs are normally used with another verb in the infinitive. This verb goes to the end of the sentence.

Wir **durften** vor dem Hotel **parken**.	*We were allowed to park in front of the hotel.*
Sie **mochte reiten**.	*She liked riding.*
Sie **mussten** eine Stunde **warten**.	*They had to wait an hour.*
Er **sollte** das Auto **waschen**.	*He was supposed to wash the car.*
Ich **wollte** neue Schuhe **kaufen**.	*I wanted to buy some new shoes.*

exercise

1 Complete the letter with suitable verbs from the box. You will need to use one verb twice.

Berlin, den 2. April

Liebe Martina,

ich **a** _____ letzte Woche schreiben, aber ich hatte keine Zeit. Mein Bruder Michael und ich **b** _____ vor zwei Wochen in Urlaub fahren, aber er war krank. Deshalb **c** _____ wir zu Hause bleiben. Michael **d** _____ im Bett bleiben. Er hatte Halsschmerzen und **e** _____ nicht reden! Er **f** _____ auch nichts essen. Ich komme dich bald besuchen.

Deine Katrin

---

sollen	können	dürfen	müssen	wollen

The future tense is used to describe what is going to happen in the future.

Sebastian **wird** im Juli in die Alpen **fahren**. *Sebastian is going (to drive) to the Alps in July.*

A The future tense is formed with the present tense of the verb **werden** *to become* plus an infinitive.

ich werde	wir werden
du wirst	ihr werdet
er/sie/es wird	Sie werden

Ich **werde** nächste Woche nach Paris **fliegen**.   *I'm going to fly to Paris next week.*

B The form of **werden** takes the first verb position (second idea) in the sentence. The infinitive goes to the end.

Sie **werden** Tennis **spielen**.   *They are going to play tennis.*

Wir **werden** am Montag auf der Messe in Basel **sein**.   *We are going to be at the trade fair in Basel on Monday.*

C In German, the present tense is often used to talk about future plans. In English, we use the present continuous.

Morgen Abend **gehen** wir ins Kino.

We're going to the cinema tomorrow evening.

exercises

1 Complete the sentences with the correct form of werden.

E.g. Ich _____ Samstagabend ins Theater gehen. →
Ich werde Samstagabend ins Theater gehen.

a Oliver und Birgit _____ im Sommer nach Italien fliegen.
b Ich _____ heute Abend Tanja besuchen.
c _____ du heute Nachmittag mitkommen?
d Erika _____ im Dezember eine Prüfung machen.
e Wir _____ übermorgen in der Stadt einkaufen.

2 What will Herr Rainer be doing next Tuesday?

E.g. Herr Rainer wird um 09.00 Uhr zum Flughafen fahren.

DIENSTAG	
09.00	zum Flughafen fahren
a 11.15	nach Rom fliegen
b 12.00	Herrn Sachs treffen
c 14.00	auf die Messe gehen
d 18.00	mit Frau Antonio essen
e 21.00	ins Theater gehen

Reflexive verbs are for describing a person or a thing doing something to himself/herself or itself.

A Reflexive verbs are made up of a main verb and a reflexive pronoun.

subject	verb	reflexive pronoun	
Ich	wasche	mich	*I wash myself*

B The accusative reflexive pronouns are **mich, dich, sich, uns, euch** and **sich**.

sich duschen *to shower (oneself)/have a shower*	
ich dusche **mich**	wir duschen **uns**
du duschst **dich**	ihr duscht **euch**
er/sie/es duscht **sich**	sie duschen **sich**
	Sie duschen **sich**

C Some verbs are reflexive in German but not in English: sich **beeilen** *to hurry*; sich **entschuldigen** *to apologise*; sich **freuen auf** *to look forward to*; sich **interessieren für** *to be interested in*; sich **kämmen** *to comb one's hair*; sich **rasieren** *to shave*; sich **schminken** *to put on one's make-up*; sich **treffen** *to meet*.

D With separable verbs, the separable prefix goes to the end of the sentence.

sich <u>an</u>ziehen → Er zieht sich <u>an</u>. *He gets dressed.*

sich <u>aus</u>ziehen → Ich ziehe mich <u>aus</u>. *I get undressed.*
sich <u>um</u>ziehen → Wir ziehen uns <u>um</u>. *We get changed.*

E If you use a reflexive verb with a part of the body or an article of clothing, you use a dative reflexive pronoun. These are the same as the accusative reflexive pronouns except for the *I* and *you* forms.

ich → **mir**

Ich putze **mir** die Zähne.   *I clean my teeth.* (lit. *I clean to me the teeth*)

du → **dir**

Du ziehst **dir** ein Hemd an.   *You put on a shirt.*

exercises

1 Add the correct reflexive pronoun to each sentence.

E.g. Ich ziehe _____ aus. (sich ausziehen) → Ich ziehe mich aus.

a Ich wasche _____. (sich waschen)
b Sie (*They*) beeilen _____ . (sich beeilen)
c Sie (*She*) freut _____ auf den Urlaub. (sich freuen)
d Er rasiert _____ jeden Morgen. (sich rasieren)
e Wir treffen _____ am Bahnhof. (sich treffen)
f Du wäschst _____ die Hände. (sich waschen)

2 Describe what Elke does every morning.

E.g. (sich duschen) Elke duscht sich.

a (sich die Zähne putzen)   c (sich das Haar kämmen)
b (sich anziehen)   **d** (sich schminken)

In conditional sentences, German uses wenn to express the English if.

Wenn es morgen sonnig ist, gehen wir reiten. *If it's sunny tomorrow, we'll go riding.*

A Conditional sentences have a **wenn** clause and a main clause, which are separated by a comma.

wenn clause	main clause	
Wenn du **kommst,**	**spielen** wir Tennis.	*If you come, we'll play tennis.*

B If you want to say that something will probably happen in the future, you use the present tense in the **wenn** clause and the present or future tense in the main clause.

wenn + present	present	*If it rains*
Wenn es morgen **regnet,**	gehe ich ins Kino.	*tomorrow, I'll*
wenn + present	future	*go to the*
Wenn es morgen regnet,	**werde** ich ins Kino gehen.	*cinema.*

C In the **wenn** clause, the verb goes to the end. The main clause starts with the verb and the subject is the second idea. In the future tense, the second verb (infinitive) goes to the end.

wenn clause	main clause	
Wenn ich Zeit **habe,**	**werde** ich Ruth **besuchen.**	*If I have time, I'll visit Ruth.*

The German word **wenn** means both *if* and *when(ever)*.

> **Wenn** ich frühstücke, trinke ich Kaffee.　　*If/When I have breakfast, I drink coffee.*

exercises

1 **Match up the two halves of the sentences and underline the verbs.**

a Wenn es regnet ...

b Wenn du kommst ...

c Wenn er morgen Zeit hat ...

d Wenn ich heute zu Hause bin ...

1 ... macht er eine Fahrradtour.

2 ... **gehe ich ins Museum.**

3 ... werde ich kochen.

4 ... werden wir Tischtennis spielen.

2 **Put each sentence into the right order, starting with wenn.**

E.g. besuche/ich/habe /Zeit/wenn/ich/meine Oma →
　　Wenn ich Zeit habe, besuche ich meine Oma.

a er/kommt/verpasst/zu spät/den Zug/wenn/er

b ich/werde/eine Jacke/wenn/habe/Geld/kaufen/ich

c sie/kommt/wenn/nach/wir/Kuchen/Hause/essen/werden

The second type of conditional sentence in German expresses greater uncertainty about a situation.

A Unreal or unfulfilled conditions are expressed with the 'subjunctive 2' form of the verb or by **würde(n)** + infinitive.

Note the word order after **wenn**.

wenn clause	subjunctive 2	infinitive	
Wenn ich Geld **hätte**,	**würde** ich ein Ferienhaus	kaufen	*If I had money, I would buy a holiday home.*

B The subjunctive 2 is formed by taking the stem of the **er/sie/es** form of the simple past tense, adding the endings **-e, -est, -e -en, -et, -en, -en**, and adding an umlaut (**ä, ö, ü**) to the vowels (**a, o** or **u**) in the stem.

werden *to become*	
ich würd**e**	wir würd**en**
du würd**est**	ihr würd**et**
er/sie/es würd**e**	sie würd**en**
	Sie würd**en**

C Other subjunctive 2 forms:

    haben → ich **hätte** *I would have*   sein → ich **wäre** *I would be*
    gehen → ich **ginge** *I would go*   kommen → ich **käme** *I would come*

Wenn er reich **wäre**, würde er zwei Autos **kaufen**.

If he (would be) were rich, he would buy two cars.

exercises

1 What would Jürgen and Erike do if they came to Freiburg?

E.g. das Münster besichtigen → Wenn sie nach Freiburg kämen, würden sie das Münster besichtigen.

a ein Weinfest besuchen
b in den Schwarzwald fahren
c die Stadt besichtigen
d den Markt besuchen
e ins Theater gehen

2 Where would they go if they had time?

E.g. Julia/Italien → Wenn Julia Zeit hätte, würde sie nach Italien fahren.

a er/nach Frankreich
b ich/nach China
c wir/nach Dänemark
d Marion/nach Indien

3 What would you do if you had money?

E.g. ein Auto kaufen → Wenn ich Geld hätte, würde ich ein Auto kaufen.

a in Urlaub fahren
b eine Wohnung kaufen
c nach Australien fliegen
d ein Boot kaufen

Polite requests, like unreal conditions, use the subjunctive 2 form of the verb.

A The verbs **haben**, **mögen**, **können** and **werden** are often used to express a polite request.

Ich **hätte** gern einen Kaffee.   *I'd like a coffee.*

B The formation of the subjunctive 2 is described in Unit 36. Here is the subjunctive 2 of **können**:

können *to be able to, can*	
ich k**ö**nn**te**	wir k**ö**nn**ten**
du k**ö**nn**test**	ihr k**ö**nn**tet**
er/sie/es k**ö**nn**te**	sie k**ö**nn**ten**
	Sie k**ö**nn**ten**

Könnten Sir mir bitte **helfen**?   *Could you help me, please?*
Könntest du mir bitte die   *Could you give me the*
  Schere **geben**?   *scissors?*

C mögen *to like*
Ich **möchte**...   *I would like...*
Möchtest du eine Tasse Tee?   *Would you like a cup of tea?*
Ich **möchte** zwei Kilo Bananen.   *I'd like two kilos of*
                                        bananas.

D werden *to become*
Ich **würde**...   I would...

Würden Sie bitte die Tür aufmachen?	*Would you open the door, please?*

E **haben** *to have*
Ich **hätte**...

Wenn ich reich **wäre**, **hätte** ich ein großes Haus.

I would have...

If I were rich, I would have a big house.

hätte + **gern** means *would like:*

Ich **hätte gern** ein Stück Kuchen. *I'd like a piece of cake.*

exercise

1 **What would they like to eat?**

E.g. Starters
Ich hätte gern Tomatensuppe.
Michael möchte Tomatensalat.

Main Course
a Ich ...
b Michael ...

Dessert
c Ich ...
d Michael ...

SPEISEKARTE

Vorspeisen
Tomatensuppe
Tomatensalat

Hauptgerichte
Rinderrouladen
Hühnerfrikassee

Desserts
gemischtes Eis
Apfelstrudel

Some expressions in German use the es form of the verb as an impersonal subject in the sentence.

A The expression **es gibt** *there is/there are* is followed by the accusative case.

Es gibt einen Supermarkt (*m.*).	*There is a supermarket.*
Es gibt zwei Banken (*pl.*).	*There are two banks.*

B Some weather expressions use **es** *it* as the subject.

es regnet *it's raining*	es friert *it's freezing*
es donnert *it's thundering*	es blitzt *it's lightning*
es schneit *it's snowing*	es ist kalt *it's cold*
es ist nebelig *it's foggy*	es ist windig *it's windy*

C Other expressions with **es**:

Wie geht es dir/euch/Ihnen?	*How are you?*
Es macht nichts.	*It doesn't matter.*
Es tut mir Leid.	*I'm sorry.*
Es tut mir weh.	*It hurts (me).*
Es geht mir gut/schlecht.	*I'm well/not well.*
Es schmeckt mir gut/nicht.	*I like/don't like it.* (taste)
Es passt/steht mir gut.	*It fits/suits me.*
Es macht Spaß.	*It's fun.*
Es gefällt mir (nicht).	*I (don't) like it.*
Es ist mir egal.	*I don't mind.*
Es ist mir warm/kalt.	*I'm hot/cold.*

D The dative personal pronouns **mir** (*me*), **dir** (*you*), **ihm** (*him*), **ihr** (*her*), etc. change according to the person being described.

Es tut **ihm** Leid.   *He's sorry.*
Es gefällt **ihr**.   *She likes it.*

exercises

1 Make sentences with *es gibt* + accusative.

E.g. Computer (*m.*) → Es gibt einen Computer.

a Lampe (*f.*)
b Schreibtisch (*m.*)
c Stuhl (*m.*)
d Telefon (*nt.*)
e Stift (*m.*)
f Akte (*f.*)

2 What's the weather like? Translate these expressions into German.

a It's raining.
b It's windy.
c It's snowing.
d It's foggy.

A group of verbs known as separable verbs are made up of two parts: a prefix and a verb.

Ich **stehe** um 7 Uhr **auf**. *I get up at 7 o'clock.*

A A separable verb has a prefix which separates from the rest of the verb and goes to the end of the sentence.

<u>an</u>kommen *to arrive*
Der Zug **kommt** um 9.25 Uhr <u>an</u>. *The train arrives at 9.25.*

B When the verbs themselves are used on their own (without a prefix), they have a different meaning: ziehen *to pull*; <u>aus</u>ziehen *to undress*.

C Common separable prefixes are **ab-, an-, auf-, aus-, ein-, mit-, um-, zu-,** and **zurück-**.

D Useful separable verbs:

abholen *to fetch*
abfahren *to depart*
ankommen *to arrive*

einsteigen *to get in/on*
fernsehen *to watch TV*
stattfinden *to take place*

anrufen *to phone*
sich anziehen *to get dressed*
aufstehen *to get up*
aussteigen *to get out/off*

teilnehmen *to take part*
umsteigen *to change (trains, buses, etc.)*
zurückfahren *to travel back*

Herr Bock **nimmt** an dem Deutschkurs <u>teil</u>.

Mr Bock is taking part in the German course.

exercise

1 Answer the questions using the information given.

E.g. Wann kommt der Zug an? | 20:40 | →

Der Zug kommt um 20.40 Uhr an.

a Wann fährt der Bus ab? | 11:15 |

b Wann fährt er zurück? | 15:00 |

c Wann stehst du auf? | 06:30 |

d Wann ruft sie an? | 14:00 |

e Wann kommt der Bus an? | 13:25 |

f Wann findet der Deutschkurs statt? | 19:30 |

An inseparable verb has a prefix which never separates from the rest of the verb.

A Inseparable verbs take the same endings as any other verb.
Evi **bestellt** ein Buch. *Evi orders a book.*

B Common prefixes for inseparable verbs: **be-, emp-, ent-, er-, ge-, über-, ver-** and **zer-**.

C Useful inseparable verbs:

beginnen *to begin*	**übersetzen** *to translate*
bekommen *to get, receive*	**verdienen** *to earn*
bestellen *to order*	**verkaufen** *to sell*
bezahlen *to pay*	**verlieren** *to lose*
empfehlen *to recommend*	**verstehen** *to understand*
übernachten *to stay overnight*	**wiederholen** *to repeat*

Frau Homann **verdient** €3 000 im Monat.	*Ms Homann earns €3,000 a month.*
Wir **übernachten** in einer Pension.	*We are staying the night in a guest house.*
Ich **verstehe** Sie nicht.	*I don't understand you.*
Die Bäckerei **verkauft** Brötchen.	*The baker's sells bread rolls.*
Susi **bekommt** einen Brief.	*Susi receives a letter.*

exercises

1 Match each German verb on the left with an English verb on the right.

a ich übernachte	1 *he translates*
b wir empfehlen	2 *I repeat*
c er übersetzt	3 *she receives*
d du verstehst	4 *it starts*
e ich wiederhole	5 *I stay overnight*
f sie bekommt	6 *you lose*
g ihr verliert	7 *we recommend*
h es beginnt	8 *you understand*

2 Complete each sentence with the verb in brackets in the present tense.

E.g. Ich _____ mit EC-Karte. (bezahlen) →
Ich bezahle mit EC-Karte.

a Das Theater _____ um 21 Uhr. (beginnen)

b Wir _____ Deutsch und Französisch. (verstehen)

c Die Post _____ Briefmarken. (verkaufen)

d Die Familie Lenz _____ in einem Gasthaus in Kitzbühel. (übernachten)

e Heute _____ wir Schnitzel mit Brokkoli und Pommes frites. (empfehlen)

3 Fill in the gaps with a verb in the present tense.

Julie und Richard sind Engländer. Sie fahren mit der Fähre nach Deutschland. In Hamburg a _____ sie im Hotel Möwenpick. Am nächsten Morgen b _____ Richard die Rechnung mit Kreditkarte. Mittags gehen sie in ein Restaurant. Julie c _____ gut Deutsch und sie d _____ die Speisekarte für Richard. Er e _____ das Steak.

Separable verbs are verbs with two parts. They form their past participles in a different way to other verbs in the perfect tense.

Ich **habe** mein Zimmer **aufgeräumt.** *I've tidied up my room.*
Wir **sind** um acht Uhr **aufgestanden.** *We got up at eight
o'clock.*

A Separable verbs form the past participle by adding -ge- after the separable prefix and take either a -t ending (weak verbs) or an -en ending (strong verbs).

• weak verbs: prefix + -ge- + -t ending: aufräumen → **aufg**erämt
• strong verbs: prefix + -ge- + -en ending: aufstehen →
  aufgestand**en**

B Some common separable verbs use **haben** in the perfect tense.

verb	past participle	meaning
aufräumen	**aufgeräumt**	*tidied up*
mitnehmen	**mitgenommen**	*took along*
einladen	**eingeladen**	*invited*
fernsehen	**ferngesehen**	*watched TV*

Ich **habe** Dieter **eingeladen.** *I've invited Dieter.*

C Some separable verbs use **sein** in the perfect tense.

Silvia **ist** in Frankfurt **angekommen.** *Silvia arrived in Frankfurt.*

verb	past participle	meaning
ankommen	**angekommen**	*arrived*
aufstehen	**aufgestanden**	*got up*
ein/aussteigen	**ein/ausgestiegen**	*got on/off (bus, etc.)*
umziehen	**umgezogen**	*moved (house)*
zurückfahren	**zurückgefahren**	*returned*

exercises

1 Choose a suitable prefix for each past participle.

E.g. Er ist um halb sieben _____ gestanden. →
Er ist um halb sieben *auf*gestanden.

a Ich habe Petra _____ geladen.

b Die Kinder haben ihr Zimmer _____ geräumt.

c Ich habe gestern Abend _____ gesehen.

d Frau Stärk ist in Hameln _____ gestiegen.

2 Complete the sentences with the past participle of the verbs in brackets.

E.g. Der Zug ist um 20.03 Uhr _____ . (ankommen) →
Der Zug ist um 20.03 Uhr angekommen.

a Ich bin im letzten Sommer nach Hamburg _____ . (umziehen)

b Paul hat mich zu seiner Fete _____ . (einladen)

c Ich habe heute _____ . (fernsehen)

d Laura ist um neun Uhr _____ . (aufstehen)

e Wir haben Martina nach Rom _____ . (mitnehmen)

An inseparable verb has a prefix which never separates from the rest of the verb.

Ich **habe** zwanzig Euro für die Lampe **bezahlt**. *I paid twenty Euros for the lamp.*

A Inseparable verbs form their past participles without -ge- and take either -t (weak verbs) or -en (strong verbs) as an ending:

bestellen → bestell<u>t</u> *ordered*   beginnen → begonn<u>en</u> *began*

Herr Schumacher **hat** einen Computer **bestellt**.	*Mr Schumacher has ordered a computer.*
Die Konferenz **hat** um neun **begonnen**.	*The conference began at nine.*

B A lot of inseparable verbs use **haben** in the perfect tense.

verb	past participle	meaning
bestellen	**bestellt**	*ordered*
bezahlen	**bezahlt**	*paid*
übernachten	**übernachtet**	*stayed overnight*
übersetzen	**übersetzt**	*translated*
verdienen	**verdient**	*earned*
verkaufen	**verkauft**	*sold*
beginnen	**begonnen**	*began*
bekommen	**bekommen**	*received*
entscheiden	**entschieden**	*decided*

verlieren	**verloren**	*lost*
versprechen	**versprochen**	*promised*
verstehen	**verstanden**	*understood*

Ich **habe** meinen Regenschirm **verloren.**   *I've lost my umbrella.*

exercises

1 **Complete each sentence with the past participle of the verb in brackets.**

E.g. Kirsten hat einen Blumenstrauß _____ . (bekommen) →
Kirsten hat einen Blumenstrauß bekommen.

a Was hast du _____ ? (verlieren)
b Ich habe es Jutta _____ . (versprechen)
c Wir haben in einem Hotel _____ . (übernachten)
d Wolfgang hat sein Auto _____ . (verkaufen)
e Ich habe mich noch nicht _____ . (entscheiden)
f Wie viel habt ihr für den Computer _____ ? (bezahlen)
g Ich habe einen Tisch _____ . (bestellen)

2 **Make sentences in the perfect tense.**

E.g. **Ich/den Brief/übersetzen → Ich habe den Brief übersetzt.**
a Er/€ 100,-/verdienen   d Ich/ein Paket/bekommen
b Der Film/um 20 Uhr/beginnen e Sie/im Hotel/übernachten
c Wir/ein Fahrrad/verkaufen   f Du/die Frage/verstehen?

The past perfect tense (sometimes called the pluperfect) is a past tense. It is used to describe a past event which happened before another past event.

A The past perfect tense is formed with the simple past form of **haben** or **sein** + a past participle.

Wir **hatten** Musik **gehört**.　　　*We had listened to music.*
Er **war** zu Hause **geblieben**.　　　*He had stayed at home.*

B Look at these examples of a weak and a strong verb in the past perfect.

kaufen *to buy*	
ich hatte gekauft	wir hatten gekauft
du hattest gekauft	ihr hattet gekauft
er/sie/es hatte gekauft	sie hatten gekauft
	Sie hatten gekauft

fahren *to go*	
ich war gefahren	wir waren gefahren
du warst gefahren	ihr wart gefahren
er/sie/es war gefahren	sie waren gefahren
	Sie waren gefahren

Er **hatte** einen neuen Anzug　　　*He had bought a new*
gekauft.　　　　　　　　　　　*suit.*

| Sie **waren** nach Hamburg **gefahren**. | *They had driven to Hamburg.* |

C The past perfect is often used with the subordinating conjunction **nachdem** (*after*). The perfect or simple past tense is often used in the other part of the sentence.

| **Nachdem** er **gegessen hatte**, las er die Zeitung. | *After he had eaten, he read the newspaper.* |

exercises

1 Complete the sentences in the pluperfect tense by adding the correct form of haben or sein.

E.g. Ich _____ Wein getrunken. (haben) → Ich hatte Wein getrunken.

a Er _____ Bratwurst mit Pommes gegessen. (haben)

b _____ du Konrad getroffen? (haben)

c Ich _____ in die Stadt gefahren. (sein)

d Steffi _____ zwei Briefe geschrieben. (haben)

e Martin und Bianca _____ den Film gesehen. (haben)

f Wir _____ in den Bergen gewandert. (sein)

2 Write sentences in the past perfect.

E.g. Ich / einen Pullover / kaufen → Ich <u>hatte</u> einen Pullover <u>gekauft</u>.

a Jens/nach Paris/fahren   d Annette/in Rom/bleiben

b wir/Musik/hören   e Karl und Liane/im Büro/arbeiten

c ich/meine Oma/besuchen

Some infinitives are used with zu in German.

A In German, the infinitive ends in **-en**: spiel<u>en</u> (*to play*)

The infinitive often goes to the end of the sentence.
Ich möchte Tennis **spielen**.	*I'd like to play tennis.*

B Most verbs are followed by the infinitive with **zu**.
Er **vergisst** immer das Fenster **zu schließen**.	*He always forgets to shut the window.*
Es **beginnt zu regnen**.	*It's starting to rain.*

C The expression **um ... zu** + infinitive means *in order to*.
Ich gehe zur Bank, **um** Geld **zu holen**.	*I'm going to the bank (in order) to fetch some money.*

D Sometimes infinitives don't need **zu**.

• After the modal verbs

dürfen *to be allowed to*	müssen *to have to*
können *to be able to*	sollen *to be supposed to*
mögen *to like*	wollen *to want to*

Ich **kann** heute **kommen**.	*I can come today.*
Er **will** Moni **treffen**.	*He wants to meet Moni.*

• After certain other verbs

bleiben *to stay*	kommen *to come*
fahren *to go*	lassen *to leave, let*
gehen *to go*	sehen *to see*
helfen *to help*	werden *to become*
hören *to hear*	

Ich **gehe** morgen **einkaufen**. *I'm going shopping tomorrow.*
Wir **kommen** dich **besuchen**. *We're coming to visit you.*

exercises

1 Add zu before the infinitive where necessary.

E.g. Ich will morgen ins Kino _____ gehen. →
Ich will morgen ins Kino gehen.

a Ich helfe dir _____ kochen.
b Wir können heute nicht _____ kommen.
c Er beginnt im Juli _____ arbeiten.
d Wir gehen morgen Tante Kristel _____ besuchen.
e Manfred möchte nach Hause _____ fahren.
f Ich muss jetzt _____ gehen.
g Ihr kommt uns _____ besuchen.
h Julia vergisst oft die Tür _____ schließen.

2 Why do you want to visit these places? Write sentences with um ... zu.

E.g. Ich/Ägypten/die Pyramiden besichtigen →
Ich möchte nach Ägypten fahren, um die Pyramiden zu besichtigen.

a Er/Paris/den Eiffelturm/besichtigen
b Wir/Washington/das Weiße Haus/sehen
c Sie (*She*)/Bayern/Schloss Neuschwanstein/besichtigen
d Ich/China/die Große Mauer/besichtigen
e Sie (*They*)/Moskau/den Kreml/sehen

When you tell another person what someone has said, you use reported speech.

A In spoken German, a **dass** clause introduces reported speech. In the **dass** clause, the verb goes to the end.

'Wir kommen morgen.'	*'We're coming tomorrow.'*
Sie sagen, **dass** sie morgen **kommen**.	*They say that they are coming tomorrow.*

B The personal pronouns **ich, du, er, sie, es, wir, ihr, sie, Sie** change in reported speech, but the tense doesn't.

'Ich habe Durst', **sagt** Olaf.	*'I'm thirsty', says Olaf.*
Er sagt, dass **er** Durst **hat.**	*He says that he is thirsty.*

C In more formal spoken and written German (e.g. the news, newspapers), a different verb form is often used for reported speech. This is called the subjunctive 1. The **er/sie/es** form of the verb is the most common.

	present	subjunctive 1
haben *to have*	er/sie/es **hat**	er/sie/es **habe**
sein *to be*	er/sie/es **ist**	er/sie/es **sei**

As there is usually no **dass** in reported speech with most present subjunctive verbs, the word order does not change.

'Ich bin in Berlin.'	*'I'm in Berlin.'*

Der Minister sagte, **er sei** in Berlin.   *The minister said he was in Berlin.*

'Ich habe eine Konferenz.'   *I have a conference.*
Er sagte, **er habe** eine Konferenz.   *He said he had a conference.*

exercises

1 Report these statements using a dass clause. The name of the person speaking is given in brackets.

E.g. (Sandra)   'Ich bin glücklich.' →
      Sie sagt, dass sie glücklich ist.

a (Paul)   Ich habe ein Auto.
b (Andrea und Paul)   Wir wohnen in Mühlheim.
c (Markus)   Ich bin zwanzig Jahre alt.
d (Susi)   Ich habe einen Hund und zwei Katzen.
e (Jan und Georg)   Wir spielen samstags Fußball.
f (Beate)   Ich arbeite in einem Hotel im Schwarzwald.
g (Katrin)   Ich habe einen Freund in Hamburg.
h (Martin)   Ich besuche gern Galerien in meiner Freizeit.

2 Report these statements. Use the subjunctive 1 form of the verb.

E.g. Ich bin in Amerika. → Er sagte, er sei in Amerika.

a Ich bin für eine Woche in New York.
b Ich bin im Hotel Atlantis.
c Ich habe ein Fernsehinterview.

In a passive sentence, the action is done to the subject of the verb.

A The present passive is formed with the present tense of the verb **werden** *to become* and a past participle.

ich werde	wir werden
du wirst	ihr werdet
er/sie/es wird	sie werden
	Sie werden

Das Auto **wird repariert.**   *The car is being repaired.*

The forms **er/sie/es wird** and **sie werden** are the most common in passive sentences.

Joghurt **wird** aus Milch **gemacht.** *Yoghurt is made from milk.*

Die Autos **werden** in Spanien **produziert.**   *The cars are produced in Spain.*

B Notice how the subject and the direct object change places in active and passive sentences.

• active

subject	verb	object	
Der Firma	kauft	den Wein.	*The company buys the wine.*

• passive

subject	verb	agent*	past participle	
Der Wein	ist	von der Firma	*gekauft.*	*The wine is bought by the company.*

Von + noun (who or what the action is done *by*) is called the 'agent'.

C The subject **man** *one* is sometimes used with an active verb (in the **er/sie/es** form) as an alternative to the passive.

• passive

Autos **werden** in Wolfsburg **gebaut.** *Cars are built in Wolfsburg.*

• active

Man **baut** Autos in Wolfsburg. *One builds cars in Wolfsburg.*

exercise

1 Where are these items sold? Write sentences in the present passive.

Zeitungen		auf dem Markt	
a Bananen		im Musikcenter	
b Jacken	werden	im Fotogeschäft	verkauft.
c Filme		am Kiosk	
d CDs		im Modegeschäft	

E.g. **Zeitungen werden am Kiosk verkauft.**

The simple past form of the passive is often used to describe past events.

Das Rathaus **wurde** 1790 **gebaut.** *The town hall was built in 1790.*

A The past passive is formed with the simple past of the verb **werden** *to become* and the past participle.

ich wurde	wir wurden
du wurdest	ihr wurdet
er/sie/es wurde	sie wurden
	Sie wurden

Das Fenster **wurde geputzt.**	*The window was cleaned.*
Die Autos **wurden** in Japan **verkauft.**	*The cars were sold in Japan.*

B The past participle goes to the end of the passive sentence.

Das Schloss wurde 1850 **gebaut.**	*The castle was built in 1850.*

C The person or thing that does the action is called the 'agent'. It is introduced with **von** *by*. The preposition **von** is followed by the dative case in German.

Das Auto wurde **von dem** Mechaniker repariert.	*The car was repaired by the mechanic*
Das Buch wurde **von** Goethe geschrieben.	*The book was written by Goethe.*

exercises

1 Complete the sentences with the correct form of the verb **werden**. All the sentences are in the past passive.

E.g. Die Frau _____ gestern verletzt. →
Die Frau wurde gestern verletzt.

a Das Auto _____ repariert.
b Die Autos _____ in Wolfsburg gebaut.
c Der Wein _____ nach Frankreich verkauft.
d Die Weine _____ in Italien produziert.

2 Write sentences using the past passive to say when the buildings were built.

E.g. das Hotel/1980 → Das Hotel wurde 1980 gebaut.

a der Bahnhof/1902
b das Theater/1893
c das Schloss/1520
d der Palast/1874
e das Museum/1934
f die Kirche/1487
g das Kloster/1350

A pronoun is a word which replaces a noun.

A

singular	plural
ich *I*	wir *we*
du *you*	ihr *you*
er *he/it*, sie *she/it*, es *it*	sie *they*
Sie *you*	Sie *you*

B There are three ways of saying *you* in German.

- **du** is the singular, familiar form used for one friend, one member of the family, one child or one animal. Nowadays, young people usually address each other in the **du** and **ihr** forms.
- **ihr** is the plural form of **du**. The plural familiar form is used for friends, members of the family, children and animals.
- **Sie** is the singular and plural formal form for *you*. It is used for people you do not know well and older people. It is always written with a capital letter.

C • **er** means *he* and *it* for masculine words.

Jörg ist im Büro. **Er** arbeitet.   *Jörg is in the office. He is working.*

- **sie** (sing.) means *she* and *it* for feminine words.

Sara wohnt in Berlin, aber **sie** kommt aus Bonn.   *Sara lives in Berlin but she comes from Bonn.*

Die Jacke ist neu. Sie ist schön. *The jacket is new. It's lovely.*

- es means *it* for neuter words.

Das Haus ist groß. Es hat zehn Zimmer. *The house is big. It has ten rooms.*

D Verbs take different endings, according to their subject, which is often referred to with a personal pronoun. Here are the present-tense endings with their respective pronouns.

ich	-e	wir	-en
du	-st	ihr	-t
er/sie/es	-t	sie	-en
		Sie	-en

exercises

1 Replace the person in bold type with a personal pronoun.

E.g. **Frau Hahn** ist im Büro. → Sie ist im Büro.

a **Herr Munz** ist zu Hause.

b **Laura und ich** gehen in die Stadt.

c **Hans und Peter** arbeiten in Berlin.

d **Meine Freundin** wartet vor dem Haus.

2 Replace the nouns in bold type with a personal pronoun.

E.g. **Das Hotel** ist in Cuxhaven. → Es ist in Cuxhaven.

a **Die Kirche** ist sehr alt.   c **Der Kuchen** schmeckt gut.

b **Das Haus** ist in der Stadt.   d **Die CD** ist super.

Personal pronouns also have an accusative form. The accusative pronoun is the direct object in the sentence.

Sie trifft **ihn** im Cafe.　　　　*She meets him in the café.*

A Personal pronouns in the nominative and accusative cases.

nom. (subject)	acc. (object)
ich *I* du *you* er *he, it,* sie *she, it,* es *it* wir *we* ihr *you* sie *they* Sie *you*	mich *me* dich *you* ihn *him, it,* sie *her, it,* es *it* uns *us* euch *you* sie *them* Sie *you*

Ich liebe **dich**.　　　　　　　　*I love you.*
Daniel besucht **mich**.　　　　　*Daniel is visiting me.*
Ich habe **euch** gesehen.　　　　*I saw you.*
Ich kaufe ihn (**der** Pullover).　*I'll buy it (the pullover).*
Ich trinke **sie** gern (**die** Cola).　*I like drinking it (the coke).*

B After prepositions which take the accusative case (Unit 54), accusative pronouns are used.

Ich habe eine Karte **für dich**.　*I have a ticket for you.*
Er fährt **ohne mich**.　　　　　　*He goes without me.*

exercises

1 Match up the nominative and accusative pronouns.

a	ich	1	Sie
b	er	2	uns
c	du	3	sie
d	sie	4	**mich**
e	Sie	5	ihn
f	wir	6	sie
g	sie	7	euch
h	ihr	8	dich

2 Replace the words in bold with an appropriate pronoun.

E.g. Ich sehe Gregor morgen. → Ich sehe ihn morgen.

a Wir treffen **Ursula** vor dem Bahnhof.

b Ich habe ein Geschenk für **Olaf**.

c Ich muss ohne **meine Eltern** fahren.

d Wann möchtest **du und Petra** essen?

e Hast du **die Katze** gesehen?

3 Complete each answer with a pronoun in the accusative case.

a Axel, hast du **die Fahrkarte**? Nein, ich finde _____ nicht.

b Wo hast du **Ella** gesehen? Ich habe _____ im Park gesehen.

c Kennt ihr **Herrn Kopf**? Ja, wir kennen _____ gut.

d Ich mag **das Eis** nicht. Ich mag _____ auch nicht.

e Ich will mit **Karl** reden. Ich rufe _____ an.

f Hast du die **Schuhe** gesehen? Nein, zeig _____ mir

g Wann schicken Sie **den Brief**? Ich schicke _____ morgen.

Personal pronouns also have a dative case form.

A The dative case pronouns are used to show the indirect object in a sentence.

nom. (subject)	dat. (ind. obj.)
ich *I*	mir *(to) me*
du *you*	dir *(to) you*
er *he, it,* sie *she, it,* es *it*	ihm *(to) him, it,* ihr *(to) her, it,* ihm *(to) it*
wir *we*	uns *(to) us*
ihr *you*	euch *(to) you*
sie *they*	ihnen *(to) them*
Sie *you*	Ihnen *(to) you*

B After prepositions which take the dative case (Unit 55), dative pronouns are used.

Ich habe ein Foto **von ihr.** *I have a photo of her.*

Dative pronouns are used after verbs which take the dative case: danken *to thank,* geben *to give,* helfen *to help.*

Ich **danke dir.** *I thank you.*

C After impersonal verbs with **es** dative pronouns are used. The pronoun changes according to the person being referred to.

Wie geht es **dir/euch/Ihnen?** *How are you?*
Es tut **mir** Leid. *I'm sorry.*
Es gefällt **ihm.** *He likes it.*

exercises

1 Fill in the missing nominative and dative personal pronouns.

nom.	dat.	nom.	dat.
sie (*she*)	ihr		
a ich	_____	e _____	Ihnen
b er	_____	f ihr	_____
c _____	dir	g sie (*they*)	_____
d wir	_____	h _____	ihm

2 Complete the sentences with a pronoun from the box.

ihnen	euch	ihm	ihr	mir	ihm

E.g. **Wohnt er bei dir? Ja, er wohnt bei <u>mir</u>.**

a Hilfst du **Mutti** in der Küche? Ja, ich helfe _____ .

b Ich gebe **Franz** eine Uhr zum Geburtstag. Das gefällt _____ .

c Wir zeigen **Anja und Mara** die Fotos. Wir zeigen _____ die Fotos.

d Ich danke **meinem Freund** für die Blumen. Ich danke _____ .

e Fährst du mit **uns** zum Weinfest? Ja, ich komme mit _____ .

3 Translate the phrases into German. Use the personal pronoun in the dative case for the word in italics.

E.g. *I* like it. → Es gefällt *mir*.

a *He* is sorry.

b *We* like it

c How are *you*? (a friend)

d *They* are sorry.

e *She* likes it.

f How are *you*? (a stranger)

A relative clause is part of a sentence which refers back to information in the main part of the sentence. The relative clause contains a relative pronoun.

A Unlike English, German can never leave out the relative pronoun.

Der Mann, der in Köln wohnt, ist sehr reich.

The man who/that lives in Cologne is very rich.

Gib mir **die Jacke, die** ich in Rom gekauft habe.

Give me the jacket, (which/that) I bought in Rome.

B Relative pronouns in German change in the different cases. The endings are the same as the definite article (**der, die, das**) endings apart from the genitive (singular and plural) and the dative plural.

	masculine	feminine	neuter	plural
nom.	der	die	das	die
acc.	den	die	das	die
dat.	dem	der	dem	denen
gen.	dessen	deren	dessen	deren

C The relative pronoun and the noun it refers back to have the same gender (*m.*, *f.* or *nt.*). The case depends on the function of the relative pronoun in the relative clause. In the following examples, the relative clauses are in square brackets.

Der Wein, [**den** wir getrunken haben,] kommt aus Spanien.	*The wine [(which) we've drunk] comes from Spain.*
Die Kinder, [**deren Mutter** im Büro ist,] sind im Kindergarten.	*The children, [whose mother is at the office,] are at kindergarten.*

In the first example, **den** represents the accusative object in the relative clause. In the second, **deren** is the genitive showing possession (*whose*).

D The verb(s) go to the end of the relative clause. If there is a preposition in the relative clause, it comes before the relative pronoun, which takes the case appropriate to that preposition (e.g. **mit** + dative).

Die Frau, **mit der** ich telefoniere, ist Architektin.	*The woman (who) I'm phoning is an architect.*

exercise

1 Make sentences about the family with the relative pronouns referring to the subject in the nominative case.

E.g. der Bruder/Köln/Elektriker →
   Der Bruder, der in Köln wohnt, ist Elektriker.

a Die Schwester/Aachen/Studentin
b Der Onkel/Kiel/Programmierer
c Die Tante/Hamm/Hausfrau
d Das Kind/Kaiserslautern/Schülerin
e Die Cousine/Hannover/Friseurin
f Der Neffe/Hamburg/Grafiker

53 prepositions and cases

Prepositions, words which describe relationships between people or things, take a certain case in German.

A In German, most prepositions take either the accusative or dative case. You need to know the gender (masculine, feminine or neuter) of the noun which comes after the preposition to be able to use the correct article. For example, the preposition **für** takes the accusative case, and the preposition **mit** takes the dative.

- **der Manager** (*m.*) → **für den Manager** (*m. acc.*)
  Ich schreibe Briefe für   *I write letters for the manager.*
  den Manager.

- **der Zug** (*m.*) → **mit dem** Zug (*m. dat.*)
  Ich fahre mit dem Zug.   *I travel by train.*

B After prepositions which take the accusative case (**für**, etc.) **der**, **die**, **das** and **dieser**, etc. and **ein**, **eine**, **ein** and **mein**, **kein**, etc. have the following forms.

	m.	f.	nt.	pl.	m.	f.	nt.	pl.
nom.	der	die	das	die	ein	eine	ein	keine
acc.	den	die	das	die	einen	eine	ein	keine

C After prepositions which take the dative case (**mit**, etc.), **der**, **die**, **das** and **ein**, **eine**, **ein**, **kein**, etc. have the following forms.

	m.	f.	nt.	pl.	m.	f.	nt.	pl.
nom.	der	die	das	die	ein	eine	ein	keine
dat.	dem	der	dem	den	einem	einer	einem	keinen

exercises

1 Who are the presents for? Make sentences with für +
accusative case.

E.g. ein Buch/Bruder (m.) →
    Ich habe ein Buch für meinen Bruder.

a eine CD/Schwester (f.)
b Socken/Vater (m.)
c Blumen/Mutter (f.)
d ein Hemd/Onkel (m.)
e einen Teddybär/Cousine (f.)

2 Make sentences about how you travel using mit + dative
case.

E.g. der Bus → Ich fahre *mit dem* Bus

a das Schiff
b der Zug
c das Fahrrad
d die Straßenbahn
e das Flugzeug

Prepositions indicate the position of things. Some are also used in expressions of time.

A Some prepositions are always followed by the accusative:

- **bis**

  Ich bleibe **bis nächsten Montag** (m.).

  I'm staying until next Monday.

  Sie fährt **bis Bonn**.

  She's going as far as Bonn.

- **durch**

  Ich gehe **durch den Wald** (m.).

  I go through the woods.

- **für**

  Er kommt **für eine Woche** (f.).

  He's coming for a week.

- **entlang**

  Sie geht **die Straße entlang** (f.).

  She goes along the street.

- **gegen**

  Ich fuhr **gegen die Wand** (f.).

  I drove into the wall.

  Wir kommen **gegen sechs**.

  We're coming at about six.

- **ohne**

  Ich fahre **ohne meinen Bruder** (m.).

  I'm going without my brother.

- **um**

  Ich komme **um drei Uhr**.

  I'm coming at three o'clock.

  Ich laufe **um die Ecke** (f.).

  I run round the corner.

The preposition **entlang** comes after the noun, which takes accusative.

den Fluss entlang (*m.*)   *along the river*

B Der, die, das, diese, etc. and ein, kein, mein, etc. have the following accusative case forms after the prepositions listed above.

	m.	f.	nt.	pl.	m.	f.	nt.	pl.
nom.	der	die	das	die	ein	eine	ein	keine
acc.	den	die	das	die	einen	eine	ein	keine

exercises

1 Match up the prepositions.

a gegen	1 without
b um	2 for
c entlang	3 at
d bis	4 **against**
e durch	5 along
f ohne	6 until
g für	7 through

2 Insert the correct preposition of time for each sentence.

E.g. Ich werde _____ sechs Uhr zu Hause sein. →
Ich werde gegen sechs Uhr zu Hause sein.

a Ich warte _____ zehn Uhr, dann gehe ich.
b Er kommt heute Abend _____ neun Uhr.
c Wir fliegen _____ eine Woche nach Spanien.

A Some prepositions are always followed by the dative case.

- **aus**
  Ich komme **aus England**.   *I'm from England.*
  Er kommt **aus der Bank** (f.),   *He comes out of the bank.*

- **bei**
  Ich bin **bei meinem Freund** (m.).   *I'm at my friend's (house).*
  Sie wohnt **bei Berlin**.   *She lives near Berlin.*

- **gegenüber**
  Das Cafe ist **gegenüber dem Kino**. (nt.)   *The cafe is opposite the cinema.*

- **mit**
  Wir fahren **mit dem Bus** (m.).   *We go by (lit. with the) bus.*

  Ich gehe **mit meiner Mutter** (f.).   *I'm going with my mother.*

- **nach**
  Sie fliegen **nach Paris**.   *They fly to Paris.*
  Ich komme **nach der Schule** (f.).   *I'll come after school.*

- **seit**
  Er wohnt **seit einem Jahr** hier (nt.).   *He's lived here for a year.*

- **von**
  Ich habe einen Brief **von meinem Bruder** (m.).   *I have a letter from my brother.*

• **zu**

  Sie geht **zum** (= zu dem) **Rathaus** (nt.). *She goes to the town hall.*

There are four prepositions which generally take the genitive case, but which often take the dative case, especially in spoken German. They are **während** *during*, **wegen** *because of*, **trotz** *in spite of* and **statt** *instead of*.

  Ich habe das Haus **statt der**   *I bought the house*
    Wohnung gekauft (f.).   *instead of the flat.*

B Der, die, das, diese etc. and ein, kein, mein, etc. have the following dative forms after the prepositions listed above.

	m.	f.	nt.	pl.	m.	f.	nt.	pl.
nom.	der	die	das	die	ein	eine	ein	keine
dat.	dem	der	dem	den	einem	einer	einem	keinen

exercise

1 Complete the sentences with a preposition from the list.

| bei | von | seit | zu | aus | mit |

a Sven kommt _____ Dänemark.
b Ich wohne in Hochdorf _____ Freiburg.
c Ich fahre _____ dem Zug.
d Martina wohnt _____ einem Monat in Bonn.
e Ich habe eine Postkarte _____ Dieter.
f Wir gehen heute Abend _____ dem Fußballmatch.

Some prepositions can be followed by either the accusative or the dative case.

A The following prepositions can take either the accusative or the dative case, depending on the context: **an, auf, hinter, in, neben, über, unter, vor** and **zwischen**.

preposition	meaning (acc.)	meaning (dat.)
an	*(go) up to, over to, onto*	*on, at*
auf	*onto*	*on, at*
hinter	*(go) behind*	*behind*
in	*into*	*in*

B When there is movement in a particular direction, the accusative case is used. When there is no movement the dative case is used.

- Accusative:
  Er fährt **in die Stadt** (f.).   *He drives into town.*

- Dative:
  Er ist **in der Stadt** (f.).   *He is in town.*

Die Maus läuft **an den Käse** (m.).
The mouse runs towards the cheese.

Die Maus geht **hinter den Käse.**
The mouse goes behind the cheese.

Die Maus sitzt **hinter dem Käse.**
The mouse is sitting behind the cheese.

exercise

1 Make sentences. Say where you are going *into* (acc. case) and where you *are* (dat. case).

E.g. die Post → Ich gehe in *die Post.* (acc.)
　　　　　　　Ich bin in *der Post.* (dat.)

a die Bäckerei
b der Bahnhof
c das Kino
d der Supermarkt
e die Stadt

f das Theater
g das Haus
h der Garten
i die Küche
j das Wohnzimmer

A closer look at four prepositions which can take either the accusative or the dative case, depending on the context.

A These prepositions can be followed by either the accusative or the dative case: **neben, über, unter, vor, zwischen**.

B

preposition	meaning (acc.)	meaning (dat.)
neben	*(go)beside, next to*	*next to, near*
über	*(go) over, across*	*over, above*
unter	*(go) under*	*under*
vor	*(go) in front of*	*in front of*
zwischen	*(go) between*	*between*

C The accusative case is used when movement is involved, the dative case to show position.

• Accusative:
Der Zug fährt **über die Brücke** (f.).   *The train goes over the bridge.*

• Dative:
Die Ampel hängt **über der Straße**.   *The traffic lights are above the road.*

Die Frau steht **vor dem Reisebüro** (nt.).
The woman is standing in front of the travel agent's.

Die Krankenschwester steht **neben dem Bett.** (nt.)
The nurse is standing next to the bed.

exercises

1 Complete the description of the living room with the dative form of der, die or das.

a Die Lampe hängt über _____ Tisch (m.).

b Das Sofa ist neben _____ Fenster (nt.).

c Der Fernseher steht vor _____ Wand (f.).

d Der Sessel ist zwischen _____ Tisch (m.) und _____ Regal (nt.).

e Ein Buch liegt unter _____ Tisch (m.).

2 Complete each sentence with either the accusative or dative form of der, die, or das.

a Ich fahre über **die/der** Brücke (*f.*).

b Das Auto fährt unter **die/der** Brücke (*f.*).

c Der Hund sitzt vor **der/dem** Stuhl (*m.*).

d Der Igel läuft vor **das/dem** Auto (*nt.*).

e Die Katze schläft unter **den/dem** Tisch (*m.*).

f Das Auto steht zwischen **dem/das** Haus (*nt.*) und **der/dem** Garten (*m.*).

g Der Park ist neben **die/der** Metzgerei (*f.*).

h Das Flugzeug fliegt über **die/den** Berge (*pl.*).

Some prepositions and articles are usually combined to make one word.

Wir gehen heute Abend **ins** Kino.	*We're going to the cinema this evening.*

The following groups are the most important preposition and article combinations.

A Prepositions in accusative case with neuter (**das**) words: auf das → aufs *onto the*; an das → ans *towards the*; in das → ins *into the*

Ich fahre **aufs Land**.	*I'm going to the country.*
Sie fahren **ans Meer**.	*They are going to the seaside.*
Wir gehen **ins Theater**.	*We're going to the theatre.*

B Prepositions with dative masculine (**der**) and neuter (**das**) words: an dem → am *on the*; bei dem → beim *at the*; in dem → im *in the*; von dem → vom *from the*; zu dem → zum *to the*

Ich sitze **am Schreibtisch**.	*I'm sitting at the desk.*
Er ist **beim Bäcker**.	*He's at the baker's.*
Sie ist **beim Tierarzt**.	*She is at the vet's.*
Daniela ist **im Zug**.	*Daniela is on the train.*
Er kommt **vom Büro** zurück.	*He comes back from the office.*
Ich gehe **zum Markt**.	*I'm going to the market.*

C Prepositions in dative case with feminine (**die**) words: zu der → zur *to the*.

Sie fährt **zur** Post.   *She drives to the post office.*

exercises

1 Complete the sentences with the short form of the words in brackets.

E.g. Sie gehen (in das) _____ Schwimmbad. →
Sie gehen *ins* Schwimmbad.

a Wir fahren (an das) _____ Meer.
b Ich komme (von dem) _____ Schwimmbad.
c Er steigt (auf das) _____ Fahrrad.
d Martina ist (bei dem) _____ Friseur.
e Ich bin (in dem) _____ Büro.
f Wir fahren (zu dem) _____ Supermarkt.
g Er geht (in das) _____ Restaurant.

2 Make sentences. Use zum or zur.

E.g. Ich fahre _____ (die Tankstelle). → Ich fahre zur Tankstelle.

a Ich gehe _____ (der Friseur).
b Er geht _____ (das Hotel).
c Wir gehen _____ (die Post).
d Du gehst _____ (der Supermarkt).
e Sie geht _____ (die Metzgerei).
f Ich gehe _____ (die Schule).
g Sie gehen _____ (der Bahnhof).

There are some everyday phrases which include a preposition.

A When prepositions are used in certain phrases, they often have different meanings. **zu** normally means *to*, but look at these examples:

Ich gehe **zum Friseur**.	*I go to the hairdresser's.*
Ich gehe **zu Fuß**.	*I go on foot.*
Ich bin **zu Hause**.	*I'm at home.*

B Here are some useful phrases with prepositions.

Ich fahre **mit dem Bus**.	*I go by car.*
Er geht **zu Fuß**.	*He goes on foot.*
Ich fahre **ins Ausland**.	*I go abroad.*
Sie ist **im Ausland**.	*She is abroad.*
Er ist **in/im/auf Urlaub**.	*He is on holiday.*
Sie ist **auf Dienstreise**.	*She's on a business trip.*
Er fährt **aufs Land**.	*He goes to the country(side).*
Sie wohnen **auf dem Lande**.	*They live in the country.*
Wir sind **zu Hause**.	*We are at home.*
Ich gehe **nach Hause**.	*I'm going home.*
Sie ist **bei mir**.	*She's at my house.*
am Sonntag	*on Sunday*
am Wochenende	*at the weekend*
zu Weihnachten	*at Christmas*
zu Ostern	*at Easter*
vor einer Woche	*a week ago*

Sag es **auf Deutsch!**   *Say it in German!*

bei gutem/schlechtem Wetter   *in good/bad weather*

exercises

1 Match up the English and German phrases.

a *in good weather*
b *in German*
c *on Tuesday*
d *on holiday*
e *at Easter*
f *in the country*
g *two weeks ago*

1 vor zwei Wochen
2 auf dem Lande
3 zu Ostern
4 **bei gutem Wetter**
5 auf Urlaub
6 auf Deutsch
7 am Dienstag

2 Choose a phrase from the list to complete each sentence.

a _____ wollen wir Ski fahren.
b Ich bin nächste Woche _____ in Kairo.
c Er fährt zum Bauernhof _____ .
d _____ bringt der Osterhase Eier!
e _____ gehen wir in die Kirche.
f Es ist Mitternacht. Ich fahre jetzt _____ .
g Ich gehe _____ , weil mein Fahrrad kaputt ist.

> am Sonntag
> zu Weihnachten
> in Urlaub
> zu Fuß
> nach Hause
> zu Ostern
> aufs Land

3 Translate these phrases into German.

E.g. *We are on holiday.* → Wir sind im Urlaub.

a a week ago
b He's at home.
c She's going home.

d He's going abroad.
e I'm on a business trip.
f We go on foot.

Some verbs in German are followed by a preposition which takes the accusative case.

Verbs + preposition + accusative case.

• **an**
denken an *to think of*
sich erinnern an *to remember*
sich gewöhnen an *to get used to*

glauben an *to believe in*
schreiben an *to write to*

• **auf**
antworten auf *to answer*
aufpassen auf *to look after*
sich beziehen auf *to refer to*
sich freuen auf *to look forward to*

sich vorbereiten auf *to
  prepare (oneself) for*
warten auf *to wait for*

• **für**
sich bedanken für *to thank for*
sich interessieren für *to be interested in*

• **in**
sich verlieben in *to fall in love with*

• **über**
diskutieren über *to discuss*
sich freuen über *to be pleased about*

• **um**
sich bewerben um *to apply for*
bitten um *to ask for*

Er **freut sich auf** das
  Wochenende.

*He's looking forward to
  the weekend.*

Ich **bewerbe mich um** den Job. *I'm applying for the job.*
Ich **warte auf** meinen Bruder. *I'm waiting for my brother.*

Ich **bedanke mich für** das Geschenk. *Thank you for the present.*

exercises

1 Match up each verb with an appropriate preposition.

a sich bedanken
b bitten
c diskutieren
d sich verlieben
e antworten
f warten
g denken

auf	über
um	in
an	auf	für

2 Complete the sentences with the correct preposition.

E.g. Wir diskutieren _____ die Ferien. →
Wir diskutieren über die Ferien.

a Ich freue mich _____ deinen Besuch.
b Wir bitten _____ eine Antwort.
c Er antwortet _____ den Brief.
d Er bewirbt sich _____ den Job.
e Sie denkt _____ ihre Freundin.
f Sie haben _____ den Bus gewartet.
g Kannst du heute _____ die Kinder aufpassen?

Some verbs in German are followed by a preposition which takes the dative case.

The following verbs are always followed by a preposition + dative case.

- **an**
  teilnehmen **an** *to take part in*

- **aus**
  bestehen **aus** *to consist of*

- **bei**
  sich bedanken **bei** *to thank*

- **mit**
  anfangen **mit** *to start with*   diskutieren **mit** *to discuss with*
  beginnen **mit** *to start with*   sprechen **mit** *to speak to*

- **nach**
  fragen **nach** *to ask about*

- **von**
  erzählen **von** *to tell about*   sich verabschieden **von** *to
  say goodbye to*

- **zu**
  einladen **zu** *to invite to*   gratulieren **zu** *to congratulate
  on*

  Ich **erzähle** dir **von meiner**   *I'll tell you about my trip.*
  Reise.

| Er **fragt** den Manager **nach** dem Brief. | *He asks the manager about the letter.* |
| Ich möchte dich **zu meiner** Geburtstagsparty **einladen**. | *I'd like to invite you to my birthday party.* |

exercises

1 Match up each German verb with its English meaning.

a einladen zu	1 *to thank*
b diskutieren mit	2 *to tell about*
c sich bedanken bei	3 *to speak to*
d fragen nach	4 *to say goodbye to*
e gratulieren zu	5 *to start with*
f sprechen mit	6 *to congratulate on*
g teilnehmen an	7 *to ask about*
h erzählen von	8 *to take part in*
i sich verabschieden von	**9 *to invite to***
j beginnen mit	10 *to discuss with*

2 Underline the examples of verb + preposition + dative case.

E.g. Zwölf Leute <u>nehmen an der</u> Konferenz <u>teil</u>.

a Wir beginnen mit einer Diskussion.

b Ich möchte mit dem Finanzdirektor sprechen.

c Frau Thoma ist heute 35 Jahre alt. Wir gratulieren ihr zum Geburtstag.

d Sie lädt uns zu einem Glas Wein ein.

e Ich verabschiede mich von meinen Kolleginnen.

Adjectives are used to describe nouns. They describe size, colour, feelings, moods, characteristics, etc.

A When the adjective comes after the noun it is describing, it does not take an ending.

Das T-Shirt ist **weiß**.	*The T-shirt is white.*
Das Mädchen ist **krank**.	*The girl is ill.*
Der Junge ist **klein**.	*The boy is small.*

Here are some useful groups of adjectives.

- **Size**

breit *wide*	lang *long*	klein *small*
kurz *short*	dick *fat*	rund *round*
eng *narrow*	groß *big*	dünn *thin*

- **Colour**

blau *blue*	grün *green*	schwarz *black*
braun *brown*	gelb *yellow*	weiß *white*
rot *red*	lila *lilac*	

- **Characteristics/mood**

alt *old*	neu *new*
(un)intelligent *(un)intelligent*	(un)freundlich *(un)friendly*
(un)interessant *(un)interesting*	langweilig *boring*
(un)glücklich *(un)happy*	traurig *sad*

- **Appearance**

(un)attraktiv *(un)attractive*	hässlich *ugly, horrible*
hübsch *pretty*	dunkel *dark*

hell *light*   gut gebaut *well-built*
schlank *slim*

- **Weather**
  kalt *cold*   kühl *cool*   sonnig *sunny*
  warm *warm*   windig *windy*   heiß *hot*
  nebelig *foggy*   regnerisch *rainy*

exercises

1 Read this description of Karl Weber and underline all the adjectives.

Ich heiße Karl Weber. Ich bin 1,80m <u>groß</u> und blond. Ich wohne in einem Dorf in der Nähe von Hannover. Hannover ist sehr groß, aber Ricklingen ist klein und ruhig. Ich arbeite in einer Bank in der Stadtmitte. Mein Büro ist groß und modern. Meine Kollegin Frau Vollmer ist freundlich. Sie ist schlank und mittelgroß. Am Wochenende, wenn es warm und sonnig ist, arbeite ich gern in meinem Garten. Der Garten ist lang und eng.

2 Say two things about each season.

im Frühling a im Sommer b im Herbst c im Winter

E.g. **Im Frühling ist es warm und windig.**

When an adjective comes before the noun is is describing, it adds an ending.

A Adjective endings change in the different cases. They take the following endings after **der, die, das**.

	masculine	feminine	neuter	plural
nom.	der neue Wein	die schwarze Katze	das kleine Haus	die alten Männer
acc.	den neuen Wein	die schwarze Katze	das kleine Haus	die alten Männer
dat.	dem neuen Wein	der schwarzen Katze	dem kleinen Haus	den alten Männern
gen.	des neuen Weines	der schwarzen Katze	des kleinen Hauses	der alten Männer

B The adjective and the article both take endings depending on what role they play in the sentence. In the examples below, **der kleine Junge** is the subject of the sentence, so takes the nominative case; **das kleine Haus** is the direct object, so takes the accusative case; **den alten Männern** follows **mit**, so takes the dative case.

Der kleine Junge ist vier Jahre alt.   *The little boy is four years old.*

Wir haben das **kleine Haus** gekauft.   *We've bought the small house.*

Er sitzt mit **den alten Männern**.   *He's sitting with the old men.*

C You use the same adjective endings after **all-** *all*, **dies-** *this*, **jed-** *each*, **jen-** *that*, **manch-** *some*, **solch-** *such*, **welch-** *which*.

Dieser rote **Pullover** gefällt mir.   *I like this red pullover.*

exercises

1 Choose the most appropriate adjective from the box for each sentence and then add the correct adjective ending in the nominative case. Use each adjective once only.

E.g.   Der _____ Bus fährt um 23.30 Uhr. →
         Der letzte Bus fährt um 23.30 Uhr.

a Die _____ Wohnung kostet 600 Euro im Monat.

b Der _____ Kühlschrank ist kaputt.

c Die _____ Tomaten schmecken gut.

d Das _____ Restaurant macht tolle Pizzas.

e Die _____ Männer sind siebzehn Jahre alt.

f Der _____ Zug fährt 200 km pro Stunde.

2 Add the correct accusative endings to each adjective.

E.g.   Ich habe den letzt____ Zug nach Frankfurt verpasst. →
         Ich habe den letzten Zug nach Frankfurt verpasst.

a Wir haben die schwarz____ Katze im Garten gesehen.

b Wann habt ihr das neu____ Sofa gekauft?

c Ich habe den französisch____ Wein getrunken.

d Er will das rot____ Auto verkaufen.

e Wo hast du die alt____ Männer gesehen?

f Daniela isst den best____ Apfel.

The adjective takes different endings when it comes before a noun with ein, eine, ein, kein, etc.

A Adjective endings change in the different cases. The following table shows the endings after **ein, eine, ein**. The plural endings are with **keine** *no* because **ein** *a, one* only exists in the singular.

	masculine	feminine	neuter	plural
nom.	ein neuer Wein	eine schwarze Katze	ein kleines Haus	keine alten Männer
acc.	einen neuen Wein	eine schwarze Katze	ein kleines Haus	keine alten Männer
dat.	einem neuen Wein	einer schwarzen Katze	einem kleinen Haus	keinen alten Männern
gen.	eines neuen Weines	einer schwarzen Katze	eines kleinen Hauses	keiner alten Männer

B The adjective and the article both take endings depending on what role they play in the sentence. In the examples below, **einen roten Pulli** is the direct object, so takes the accusative ending; **einem neuen Schläger** follows **mit**, so takes the dative ending.

Ich habe **einen roten Pulli**. *I have a red pullover.*
Ich spiele mit **einem neuen Schläger**. *I'm playing with a new racquet.*

C The same adjective endings are used after **mein** *my*, **dein** *your*, **sein** *his*, **ihr** *her*, **unser** *our*, **euer** *your*, **Ihr** *your*, **ihr** *their*.

Ich trage **meine** blaue Jacke.   *I'm wearing my blue jacket.*

D Adjectives which end in **-a**, such as **lila** *lilac* and **rosa** *pink*, do not take adjective endings.

ein **rosa** T-Shirt   *a pink T-shirt*

exercises

1 Add the correct nominative ending to each adjective.

E.g. ein traurig_____ Mädchen (*nt.*) → ein trauriges Mädchen.

a eine lang_____ Nacht (*f.*)
b ein klein_____ Junge (*m.*)
c dein alt_____ Buch (*nt.*)
d meine neu_____ Adresse (*f.*)
e ein indisch_____ Restaurant (*nt.*)
f keine schlecht_____ Idee (*f.*)
g mein link_____ Bein (*nt.*)
h ein schön_____ Tag (*m.*)

2 Complete the description using the following information and adding the correct accusative endings to the adjectives.

E.g. Bluse (*f.*)/weiß → Susi trägt eine weiße Bluse.

a Hut (*m.*)/braun   c Rock (*m.*)/grün
b Jacke (*f.*)/gelb   d Handtasche (*f.*)/braun

An adjective adds an ending when there is no article (der, ein, etc.).

A These endings are for adjectives without **der, ein, kein, dies-,** etc. In the singular they are the same endings you use with **ein, eine, ein** + adjective except for the dative case.

	masculine	feminine	neuter	plural
nom.	neu<u>er</u> Wein	schwarz<u>e</u> Katze	klein<u>es</u> Haus	blau<u>e</u> Augen
acc.	neu<u>en</u> Wein	schwarz<u>e</u> Katze	klein<u>es</u> Haus	blau<u>e</u> Augen
dat.	neu<u>em</u> Wein	schwarz<u>er</u> Katze	klein<u>em</u> Haus	blau<u>en</u> Augen
gen.	neu<u>en</u> Weines	schwarz<u>er</u> Katze	klein<u>en</u> Hauses	blau<u>er</u> Agen

B When there is no article, the adjective adds endings which show three things:

- whether the noun is singular or plural
- the gender of the noun (masculine etc.)
- the case (nominative, accusative, etc.)

Französischer Wein schmeckt gut (m.).   *French wine tastes good.*

Französischer Wein is the subject, so takes the nominative.

Ich habe **blaue Augen** (pl.).   *I have blue eyes.*

blaue Augen is the direct object, so takes the accusative.

C These endings are also used after numbers.

Andreas hat **zwei neue**   *Andreas has two new shirts.*
Hemden (pl.).

exercises

1 Complete the newspaper advertisement by adding the correct adjective endings.

Indischer Teppich (*m.*) € 40, neu_____ Bett (*nt.*) € 80,
rund_____ , braun_____ Tisch (*m.*) € 80, alt_____
Kommode (*f.*) € 50, groß_____ Kühlschrank (*m.*) € 60
Tel. 51 12 34

2 Complete the description of Peter Hansen by adding the correct accusative endings to the adjectives.

Name:	Peter Hansen
Augen (*nt., pl.*):	**grau** **Haare** (*nt., pl.*): **kurz, braun**
Liebt:	Autos (*nt., pl.*) (**schnell**), Hunde (*m., pl.*) (**groß**)
Hasst:	Wetter (*nt.*) (**schlecht**)
Lieblingsessen:	Käse (*m.*) (**griechisch**), Eis (*nt.*) (**italienisch**)
Lieblingsgetränk:	Rotwein (*m.*) (**französisch**)

E.g. Peter Hansen hat *graue Augen.*

a Er hat …   d Er isst gern …
b Er liebt …   e Er trinkt gern …
c Er hasst …

Many expressions of greeting, for example Guten Morgen! (Good morning), include an adjective which takes an ending.

A The first part of the sentence in greetings is usually left out in both German and English.

(Ich wünsche dir/Ihnen einen)	*(I wish you a)*
Guten Morgen!	*Good morning.*

B The accusative adjective endings used after **ein, eine, ein** are added to the adjective in many greetings: -**en** in the masculine, -**e** for the feminine and -**es** for the neuter.

Gut**en** Tag (m.)!	*Good day!*
Gut**e** Nacht (f.)!	*Good night!*
Schön**es** Wochenende (nt.)!	*Have a nice weekend!*

C The following expressions all take accusative endings:

Gut**en** Abend!	*Good evening!*
Gut**en** Appetit!	*Enjoy your meal!*
Gut**e** Besserung!	*Get well soon!*
Gut**e** Fahrt!	*Have a good journey!*
Gut**en** Rutsch!	*Happy New Year (coll.)!*
Froh**es** Neues Jahr!	*Happy New Year!*
Froh**e** Weihnachten!	*Happy Christmas!*
Viel**en** Dank	*Thank you very much!*
Herzlich**en** Glückwunsch!	*Congratulations!*
Herzlich**en** Glückwunsch zum Geburtstag!	*Happy Birthday!*

D Opening and closing expressions in letters also take adjective endings.

- Informal (to friends)

Lieb**er** Daniel,	*Dear Daniel,*
Lieb**e** Julia,	*Dear Julia,*
Schön**e** Grüße,	*Best wishes,*

- Formal

Sehr geehr**te** Damen und Herren,	*Dear Sir or Madam,*
Sehr geehr**ter** Herr Lutz,	*Dear Mr Lutz,*
Sehr geehr**te** Frau Rainer,	*Dear Mrs/Ms Rainer,*
Mit freundlich**en** Grüßen,	*Yours sincerely/Yours faithfully,*

exercise

1 Match up the two halves to make greetings.

a Viel	1 Rutsch!
b Herzlichen	2 Appetit!
c Gute	3 Wochenende
d Vielen	4 Weihnachten
e Schönes	5 Dank
f Guten	6 Glückwunsch!
g Guten	7 Besserung
h Frohe	8 Spaß!

The comparative form of adjectives is used to make comparisons between people or things.

A The comparative of adjectives is formed by adding an **-er** ending to the adjective.

adjective	comparative
klein *small*	klein**er** *smaller*
interessant *interesting*	interessant**er** *more interesting*
langweilig *boring*	langweilig**er** *more boring*
leise *quiet*	leis**er** *quieter*
schnell *fast*	schnell**er** *faster*
langsam *slow*	langsam**er** *slower*
laut *loud*	laut**er** *louder*
reich *rich*	reich**er** *richer*

B Many short adjectives (of one syllable) add an umlaut to the vowel (**a, o, u**) and an **-er** ending to form the comparative.

alt → **ä**lt**er** (*older*)   hart → **hä**rt**er** (*harder*)
jung → j**ü**ng**er** (*younger*)   kalt → k**ä**lt**er** (*colder*)

Daniel ist **jünger** als Stefan.   *Daniel is younger than Stefan.*

Other adjectives which take an umlaut in the comparative are **groß** *big*, **lang** *long*, **schwach** *weak*, **stark** *strong*, **arm** *poor*, **warm** *warm*, **kurz** *short*.

C Some comparative adjectives have irregular forms:
gut *good* → **besser** *better*   hoch *high* → **höher** *higher*

D After a comparative adjective, *than* is translated by **als**.
Jan ist **jünger als** Mara.   *Jan is younger than Mara.*

(Not) as … as + adjective is translated by **(nicht) so … wie**.
Mara ist **so groß wie** Anna.   *Mara is as tall as Anna.*
Sie ist **nicht so groß wie** Tobias.   *She is not as tall as Tobias.*

exercise

1 Write down the comparative form of each adjective on the left. Then find the comparative adjective with the opposite meaning.

adjective	comparative	opposites
spät	**a** **später**	1 schneller
alt	**b** _____	2 länger
gut	**c** _____	3 **früher**
langsam	**d** _____	4 reicher
stark	**e** _____	5 schlechter
leise	**f** _____	6 jünger
interessant	**g** _____	7 lauter
arm	**h** _____	8 langweiliger
kurz	**i** _____	9 kleiner
groß	**j** _____	10 schwächer

The superlative form of the adjective is used to make comparisons like the smallest, the highest.

der **höchste** Berg   *the highest mountain*

A There are two superlative forms in German.

• When the superlative adjective comes before the noun it describes, it adds -(e)st + adjective ending.

der schnell<u>ste</u> Mann	*the fastest man*
die klein<u>ste</u> Katze	*the smallest cat*
das schön<u>ste</u> Haus	*the nicest house*
die höch<u>sten</u> Berge	*the highest mountains*

• When the superlative adjective comes after the verb **sein** *to be*, you use **am** + adjective + **-sten**.

Das Haus ist **am kleinsten**.   *The house is the smallest.*

B Many short adjectives of one syllable add an umlaut to the vowel (**a, o, u**) in the superlative form.

adjective	superlative (before noun)	superlative (after verb)
groß *big*	grö<u>ßte</u> *biggest*	**am** grö<u>ßten</u> *biggest*
hoch *high*	höch<u>ste</u> *highest*	**am** höch<u>sten</u> *highest*

Other adjectives that take an umlaut in the superlative are: **jung** *young*; **lang** *long*; **schwach** *weak*; **stark** *strong* and **warm** *warm*.

C When the adjective ends in -d, -s, -ß, -sch, -t, -x, or -z, an extra -e is added in the superlative form.

alt *old* → älteste/am ältesten *eldest*
hart *hard* → härteste/am härtesten *hardest*
kalt *cold* → kälteste/am kältesten *coldest*
kurz *short* → kürzeste/am kürzesten *shortest*

D Some adjectives have irregular superlative forms.
gut *good* → beste/am besten *best*
nah *near* → nächste/am nächsten *nearest*

exercises

1 Fill in the superlative form of the adjective.

a Ich habe die _____ CD gekauft.	(gut)
b Siehst du das _____ Gebäude?	(hoch)
c Wer ist der _____ Mann der Welt?	(alt)
d Die Maus ist das _____ Tier.	(klein)
e Der _____ Tag ist im Juni.	(lang)
f Der _____ Wein kommt aus Italien.	(gut)

2 Make two superlative forms from each adjective.

E.g. jung/der Sohn →
     der jüngste Sohn/der Sohn ist am jüngsten

a kalt/der Winter
b billig/die Karte
c klein/ die Katze
d hoch/der Turm
e gut/das Restaurant
f jung/die Frau
g kurz/der Weg

Adverbs are used to describe verbs. Most adverbs have the same form as adjectives.

Er fährt **langsam**.　　　　　　*He drives slowly.*

A An adverb describes how something is done. Most German adverbs have the same form as adjectives.

Er läuft **schnell**.	*He runs quickly* (adverb).
Er ist **schnell**.	*He is quick* (adjective with the verb **sein**).

B When making comparisons, the adverb adds an **-er** ending (like comparative adjectives). In the superlative, the **am** + adverb + **-sten** form is used (like some superlative adjectives).

adverb	comparative	superlative
früh *early*	früh**er** *earlier*	**am** früh**esten** *the earliest*
langsam *slow*	langsam**er** *slower*	**am** langsam**sten** *the slowest*
schlecht *badly*	schlecht**er** *worse*	**am** schlecht**esten** *the worst*
schnell *quickly*	schnell**er** *quicker*	**am** schnell**sten** *the quickest*
spät *late*	spät**er** *later*	**am** spät**esten** *the latest*
vorsichtig *carefully*	vorsichtig**er** *more carefully*	**am** vorsichtig**sten** *the most carefully*

Ich stehe immer **früher** auf als du.	*I always get up earlier than you.*

C Some adverbs have irregular forms.

gern *like*	→ lieber *prefer* →	am liebsten *best of all*
viel *much*	→ mehr *more* →	am meisten *most*
gut *well*	→ besser *better* →	am besten *best*

Ich spiele **lieber** Tennis. *I prefer playing tennis.*

D The superlative adverb sometimes takes first position in the sentence. The verb is second, followed by the subject.

Am liebsten arbeite ich *I like working in the*
im Garten. *garden best of all.*

exercises

1 Write sentences about Peter and Konrad.

Peter	Konrad
Ich fahre langsam.	Ich fahre schnell.
Ich gehe früh ins Bett.	Ich gehe spät ins Bett.
Ich singe gut.	Ich singe nicht sehr gut.
Ich lese nicht viel.	Ich lese viel.

E.g. (Konrad) → **Konrad fährt schneller als Peter.**

a (Peter)
b (Peter)
c (Konrad)

A sentence is made up of various parts: subject, verb, object, etc. These elements are organized in a certain order.

A In German, the subject is often the first idea in the sentence.
Das Kino ist in der Salzstraße.　　*The cinema is in Salzstraße.*

B The main verb is the second idea in a statement.
Er **arbeitet** in einem Büro.　　*He works in an office.*
Ich **habe** eine Schwester.　　*I've got a sister.*

C A time expression sometimes takes first position in a statement. The verb is the second idea and is then followed by the subject.
Gestern waren wir in Rom.　　*Yesterday we were in Rome.*

D When the sentence contains more than one adverb or adverbial phrase, the *time, manner, place* rule is followed (i.e. words or phrases that tell you *When?* come before phrases that tell you *How?*, which are in turn followed by phrases that tell you *Where?*).

Ich fahre *morgen* **mit dem Auto** <u>nach Dresden</u>.　　*I'm going to Dresden by car tomorrow.*
Heute geht Heike **früh** <u>zur Arbeit</u>.　　*Heike is going to work early today.*

In the above examples, the *time* expressions are *morgen* and *heute*, the manner expressions are **mit dem Auto** and **früh**, and the **place** expressions are <u>nach Dresden</u> and <u>zur Arbeit</u>.

E If there are two verbs in the sentence, the second verb (infinitive or past participle) goes to the end.

Er **kann** Fahrrad **fahren.**   *He can ride a bike.*
Gestern **haben** wir meine Tante   *Yesterday we visited my*
  besucht.   *aunt.*

exercises

1 Put the expressions in brackets into the sentence in the correct order using the Time, Manner, Place rule.

E.g. Ich fahre (am Dienstag/nach Leipzig/mit Lothar) →
    Ich fahre am Dienstag mit Lothar nach Leipzig.

a Der Bus fährt (nach Ulm/um 10 Uhr)
b Wir fliegen (mit Julia/nach Portugal/nächste Woche)
c Dirk war (in Spanien/für zwei Wochen)
d Ich habe (am Samstag/im Park) Tennis gespielt.

2 Complete the sentences by putting the verbs in the correct order.

E.g. Wir _____ gestern Tennis _____ . (gespielt/haben) →
    Wir haben gestern Tennis gespielt.

a Er _____ mit dem Bus _____ . (ist/gefahren)
b Ich _____ im Supermarkt Butter und Milch _____ .
  (kaufen/kann)
c Heute _____ wir meine Oma _____ . (besuchen/wollen)
d Am Sonntag _____ ich im Garten _____ . (arbeiten/werde)

Conjunctions are linking words between two sentences or clauses.

A Two independent sentences can be linked with a joining word known as a conjunction. A co-ordinating conjunction does not change the word order of the two clauses it links.

Ich spiele gern Tennis. + Er fährt gern Ski.

Ich spiele gern Tennis **und** er fährt gern Ski.

B The following are co-ordinating conjunctions.

und *and*	**oder** *or*
aber *but*	**entweder ... oder** *either ... or*
denn *because*	**sondern** *but* (with negatives)

Ich kaufe eine Torte **oder** backst du einen Kuchen? — *I'll buy a gateau or are you going to bake a cake?*

Ich arbeite heute **nicht**, **sondern** ich mache eine Radtour. — *I'm not working today but (I'm) going for a bike ride.*

C The two clauses are separated by a comma before most conjunctions (exception: **entweder ... oder**). The comma can be left out before **und** and **oder**.

Entweder ruft sie an **oder** sie schickt eine E-Mail. — *She will either telephone or send an e-mail.*

Conjunctions are also used between single words and phrases.

Ich komme **entweder** am Montag **oder** am Dienstag. — *I'll come either on Monday or on Tuesday.*

exercises

1 Make sentences.

a Ich möchte nicht schwimmen gehen,	denn	mit dem Auto.
b Ich trinke gern Kaffee	aber	Golf spielen.
c Ich wollte dich besuchen,	oder	es ist dort wärmer.
d Willst du in die Kneipe gehen	und	ich musste zur Arbeit.
e Er fliegt im Winter nach Spanien,	oder	Tee mit Milch.
f Ich fahre entweder mit dem Zug	sondern	zu Hause bleiben?

2 Complete the sentences with appropriate co-ordinating conjunctions from the box.

| entweder | oder | sondern | aber | denn |

a Er wollte spazieren gehen, _____ es regnete.
b Wir treffen uns um halb acht, _____ der Film beginnt um acht Uhr.
c Ich kaufe _____ einen Rock _____ eine Hose.
d Ich fahre nicht nach Berlin, _____ nach Potsdam.

2 Join each pair of sentences with a suitable conjunction.

E.g. Heute komme ich nicht. Ich habe keine Zeit. →
Heute komme ich nicht, denn ich habe keine Zeit.

a Wir möchten in Urlaub fahren. Wir haben kein Geld.
b Er hat kein Auto. Er hat ein Motorrad.
c Willst du nach Portugal fahren? Willst du nach Spanien fahren?

Conjunctions are linking words between two parts of a sentence. The word order in the sentence changes with subordinating conjunctions.

A When two sentence parts are joined together, one part is called the main clause and the other part, which contains the subordinating conjunction, is called the subordinate clause. They are separated by a comma.

Ich gehe heute essen, **weil** ich Geburtstag **habe**.	*I'm going out for a meal today because it's my birthday.*

B Here are some common subordinating conjunctions.

als *when (in the past)*	obwohl *although*
bevor *before*	seit *since*
bis *until*	sobald *as soon as*
dass *that*	während *while*
nachdem *after*	wenn *if, when, whenever*
ob *whether*	weil *because*

C In the subordinate clause, the verb(s) goes to the end.

Er tankt, **bevor** er nach Hamburg **fährt**.	*He fills up with petrol before he drives to Hamburg.*
Ich weiß, **dass** du letzten Freitag **geheiratet hast**.	*I know that you got married last Friday.*
Ich werde zum Park gehen, **weil** es heute sonnig **ist**.	*I'll go to the park because it's sunny today.*

D A sentence can start with the subordinate clause followed by a main clause. The main clause starts with the verb, the subject is second and the second verb (infinitive, past participle) goes to the end.

Als ich nach Hause **gekommen** *When I came home, I*
   bin, habe ich Musik **gehört.**   *listened to music.*

exercises

1 Match up each German conjunction on the left with its English meaning on the right.

a bis	**1** *that*
b sobald	**2** *before*
c ob	**3** *because*
d dass	**4** *until*
e seit	**5** *when*
f weil	**6** *as soon as*
g als	**7** *since*
h bevor	**8** *whether*

2 Make sentences with ich ... weil ...

E.g. Italien/Pisa →
     Ich fahre nach Italien, weil ich Pisa besuchen möchte.

a Frankreich/Paris
b Deutschland/Berlin
c Griechenland/Athen

Questions are often introduced with a question word.

A Question words, known as interrogatives, take first position in the sentence, followed by the verb as second idea and then the subject.

Wann gehst du nach Hause?   *When are you going home?*

Important question words

wann? *when?*	womit? *what with?*
um wie viel Uhr? *when/(at) what time?*	warum? *why?*
was? *what?*	wieso? *why?/how come?*
was für? *what kind of?*	wie? *how?/what?*
wo? *where?*	wie lange? *how long?*
wohin? *where to?*	wie viel? *how much?*
woher? *where from?*	wie viele? *how many?*
wozu? *what for?*	wer? *who?*

Wann kommst du?   *When are you coming?*

Was hast du gestern gemacht?   *What did you do yesterday?*

Was für ein Auto hast du?   *What kind of car have you got?*

Wo ist mein Schlüssel?   *Where is my key?*

Warum wartest du hier?   *Why are you waiting here?*

Wohin fahren wir?   *Where are we going (to)?*

Wie lange bleibt er in Essen?   *How long is he staying in Essen?*

exercises

1 Match up each question with a suitable answer.

a Wo arbeitest du? 1 Ich komme um sechs Uhr.
b Wer ist die Frau? 2 Es ist zehn nach sieben.
c Woher kommt er? 3 **Ich arbeite in einer Bank.**
d Wann kommst du? 4 Sie bleibt zwei Wochen.
e Wie viel Uhr ist es? 5 Sie heißt Katrin Baumann.
f Wie lange bleibt sie? 6 Er kommt aus Stuttgart.

2 Fill in the missing question words from the box.

was für	wohin	wie viel	wo	warum	was

a _____ wohnen deine Eltern?
b _____ kommst du nicht mit?
c _____ machst du heute Abend?
d _____ ein Fahrrad hast du?
e _____ gehen wir am Samstag?
f _____ kosten die Schuhe?

The question words wer (who) and welcher (which) change in the different cases.

A The question word **wer** has the following case forms.

nom.	**wer** *who?*
acc.	**wen** *who?*
dat.	**wem** *who...to? whom?*
gen.	**wessen** *whose?*

Wer ist das?	*Who is that?*
Wen hast **du** gesehen?*	*Who did you see?*

*The accusative case **wen** is used when there is an object in the sentence.

The dative case **wem** with the verb **gehören** *to belong to* is almost always used instead of the genitive case **wessen** and the verb **sein**.

Wem gehört das Buch?	*Who does the book belong to?*
(**Wessen** Buch ist das?)	*(Whose book is that?)*
Wem schneclet der Wein?	*Who likes the wine?*

	masculine	feminine	neuter	plural
nom.	welch**er**	welch**e**	welch**es**	welch**e**
acc.	welch**en**	welch**e**	welch**e**	welch**e**
dat.	welch**em**	welch**er**	welch**em**	welch**en**
gen.	welch**es**	welch**er**	welch**es**	welch**er**

B welcher *which* takes the same endings as the determiner dieser *this*.

> Welchen (m., acc.) Film möchtest du sehen?
> *Which film would you like to see?*

> Welcher (m., nom.) Pullover gefällt dir?
> *Which pullover do you like (lit. pleases you)?*

exercises

1 Complete the sentences with wer? or wen?

a _____ ist am Apparat?

b _____ hast du gesehen?

c _____ ist die Frau im roten Kleid?

d _____ willst du besuchen?

e _____ hat er getroffen?

f _____ ist im Büro?

2 Choose the correct question word from the box.

a _____ gefällt diese CD?

b _____ kommt zu unserer Party am Samstag?

c _____ hat Martina gestern Abend besucht?

d _____ gehört die Tasche?

e _____ hat morgen Zeit?

wen
wer
wem
wer
wem

3 Complete the questions with the correct form of welcher (nom. or acc.). The gender of each noun is given in brackets.

E.g. _____ Schuhe gefallen dir? (*pl.*) → *Welche* Schuhe gefallen dir?

a _____ Farbe gefällt dir? (*f.*)

b _____ Pullover gefällt dir? (*m.*)

c _____ Buch möchtest du haben? (*nt.*)

d _____ Wein trinkst du? (*m.*)

There are several ways of asking questions in German. In questions the position of the subject and the verb(s) often change.

Fährt der Bus nach Lahr?
Does the bus go to Lahr?

A With the correct intonation when speaking, a statement becomes a question.

Du **kommst** heute Abend ?   *You're coming this evening?*

B In yes/no questions, the verb takes first position and is followed by the subject.

Hast du einen Stift?   *Have you got a pen?*

C If there is a question word in the sentence, it takes first position.

Was machst du heute?   *What are you doing today?*
Warum weinst du?   *Why are you crying?*
Wo ist Frau Linke?   *Where is Frau Linke?*

D In questions with more than one verb, the second verb (infinitive, past participle) goes to the end of the sentence.

Warum willst du in die Stadt **gehen?**	*Why do you want to go to town?*
Hast du eine Zeitung **gekauft?**	*Have you bought a newspaper?*

E The question tags **nicht wahr?** and **oder?** turn a statement into a question.

Du hast Zeit, **oder?**	*You've got time, haven't you?*
Wir gehen jetzt, **nicht wahr?**	*We're going now, aren't we?*

exercise

1 Make questions.

E.g. ins Kino/willst/gehen/du → Willst du ins Kino gehen?

a du/Katrin/gesehen/hast

b fahren/wann/nach Basel/wir

c du/gestern/gekauft/was/hast

d wollen/am Samstag/was/wir/machen

e morgen/du/was/machst

f oder/du/Zeit/hast

g er/spät/so/warum/kommt

h wir/Hamburg/fahren/nach

One of the most common negative forms in German is nicht (not). Nicht is used with verbs.

A The negative **nicht** *not* can be placed in several positions in a sentence. It appears at or near the end of the sentence when the whole sentence is negated.

Ich warte **nicht**.	*I'm not waiting.*
Ich habe heute **nicht** gearbeitet.	*I haven't worked today.*

Other positions of **nicht** in a sentence:

• before a past participle or an infinitive:

Ich bin **nicht gegangen**.	*I didn't go.*
Sie hat das Kleid **nicht gekauft**.	*She hasn't bought the dress.*
Er kann heute **nicht kommen**.	*He can't come today.*

• before adjectives:

Er war **nicht krank**.	*He wasn't ill.*
Ich bin **nicht traurig**.	*I'm not sad.*

• before adverbs of manner or of place:

Ich komme **nicht mit dem Bus**.	*I'm not coming by bus.*
Er spielt **nicht gern** Schach.	*He doesn't like playing chess.*
Ich gehe **nicht zum Zahnarzt**.	*I'm not going to the dentist.*

- before a particular word or phrase for emphasis:
  Ich will **nicht mit dir** reden.   *I don't want to talk to you.*

- after the verb in command forms:
  Wein **nicht**!   *Don't cry!*
  Gehen Sie **nicht**!   *Don't go!*

exercises

1 Write sentences with nicht.

E.g. Musik hören → Oliver hört *nicht* gern Musik.

a schwimmen   d ins Kino gehen
b fotografieren   e Gitarre spielen
c joggen gehen   f kochen

2 Make the following sentences negative by adding nicht in the correct place.

E.g. Ich lese gern. → Ich lese *nicht* gern.

a Er ist gekommen.
b Gestern war es sonnig.
c Sie geht zur Uni.
d Morgen will ich in die Kirche gehen.
e Ich gehe gern spazieren.
f Er ist in der Stadt.
g Gehen Sie bitte!
h Wir wohnen in Leipzig.

Another important negative form in German is kein. It is used with nouns.

A Kein meaning *no*, *not a*, *not any*, is the negative form used before nouns. **nicht + ein** is nearly always replaced by **kein**.

Ich habe keine Schwester.	*I haven't got a sister.*
Ich möchte kein Bier.	*I don't want any beer.*

B Kein takes the same case endings as **ein**.

	masculine	feminine	neuter	plural
nom.	kein	keine	kein	keine
acc.	keinen	keine	kein	keine
dat.	keinem	keiner	keinem	keinen
gen.	keines	keiner	keines	keiner

Ich habe **keinen** Garten (m.).	*I haven't got a garden.*
Ich habe **kein** Geld (nt.).	*I haven't got any money.*
Ich habe **keinen** Hund (m.).	*I haven't got a dog.*
Ich habe **keine** Zeit (f.).	*I haven't got any time.*
Er hat **keine** Geschwister (pl.).	*He has no brothers or sisters.*

C When **kein** is used on its own, i.e. without the noun it is referring to, it takes the following endings.

	masculine	feminine	neuter	plural
nom.	keiner	keine	keins	keine
acc.	keinen	keine	keins	keine
dat.	keinem	keiner	keinem	keinen

The endings are identical with the last letter(s) of **der, die** and **das** in all the cases. The genitive form is hardly ever used.

Hast du ein Fahrrad?	*Have you got a bike?*
Nein, ich habe **keins**.	*No, I haven't got one.*

exercises

1 Put in the correct accusative form of kein.

E.g. Es gibt _____ Reis. (*m.*) → Es gibt keinen Reis.

a Es gibt _____ Milch. (*f.*)   **d** Ich habe _____ Eis (*nt.*)

b Wir haben _____ Brot. (*nt.*)   **e** Es gibt _____ Kuchen.

c Es gibt _____ Eier (*pl.*)   (*m.*)

2 Answer the questions with a negative. Use the correct accusative form of kein.

E.g. Möchtest du einen Tee? →   Nein, danke. Ich möchte keinen Tee.

Möchtest du...

a eine Schokolade?   **d** einen Wein?

b einen Kaffee?   **e** ein Stück Kuchen?

c ein Bier?   **f** einen Orangensaft?

There are a lot of phrases which refer to the present, such as heute (today).

A Time expressions often stand after the verb.

Wir fahren **heute** nach Paris.   *We are going to Paris today.*

B They are sometimes placed at the beginning of the sentence for emphasis and are followed by the verb and the subject.

Heute Nachmittag *geht er* in die Sauna.   *He's going to the sauna this afternoon.*

C Some useful expressions of present time.

heute *today*
heute früh *early today*
heute Morgen *this morning*
heute Nachmittag *this afternoon*
heute Abend *this evening*
heute Nacht *tonight*
jetzt/nun *now*
gerade *just, now*
in diesem Moment *at this moment, now*
sofort *at once*
gleich *(almost) at once, in a moment*
zur Zeit *at the present time*

Ich fahre **heute Vormittag** nach Mainz.   *I'm going to Mainz this morning.*

Was machst du **gerade**?   *What are you doing at the moment?*

Wir sehen **gerade** fern. *We're watching TV at the moment.*

Ich komme **sofort.** *I'm coming at once.*
Zur Zeit arbeite ich in Hamburg. *I'm working in Hamburg at the present time.*

exercise

1 Match each German expression on the left with its English equivalent on the right.

a **heute Abend**	1 *today*	
b gleich	2 *this afternoon*	
c heute	3 *early today*	
d gerade	4 *in a moment*	
e heute früh	5 *this morning*	
f zur Zeit	6 *at this moment*	
g sofort	7 *this evening*	
h heute Nachmittag	8 *at once*	
i in diesem Moment	9 *just now*	
j heute Morgen	10 *at the present time*	

79 time past and future

Certain expressions of time refer to the past, such as gestern (yesterday) or the future, such as morgen (tomorrow).

A The following expressions refer to the past:

vorgestern *the day before yesterday*
gestern *yesterday*
gestern Vormittag *yesterday morning*
gestern Nachmittag *yesterday afternoon*
gestern Abend *yesterday evening*
gestern Nacht *last night*
letzte Woche *last week*
letztes Jahr *last year*
vorher *before*
früher *in earlier times*
neulich *recently*

David hat uns **gestern Abend** besucht.	*David visited us yesterday evening.*
Letztes Jahr bin ich in die USA geflogen.	*I flew to the USA last year.*
Ich habe **neulich** Roland getroffen.	*I met Roland recently.*

B The following expressions refer to the future:

morgen *tomorrow*	nächste Woche *next week*
morgen Abend *tomorrow evening*	nächstes Jahr *next year*
übermorgen *the day after tomorrow*	bald *soon*
nächsten Montag *next Monday*	später *later*

Morgen werde ich arbeiten. *I'm going to work tomorrow.*

Wir essen **später**. *We're going to eat later.*

exercises

1 Match up the German time expressions with their English translations.

a vorgestern   1 *last year*
b vorher   2 *soon*
c letztes Jahr   3 *the day before yesterday*
d früher   4 *before*
e bald   5 *in earlier times*

2 Today is Friday. Look at Roland's diary and say what he is going to do over the next few days, starting each answer with a time expression from the box.

| nächsten Montag | ~~morgen Vormittag~~ |
| morgen Abend | übermorgen | morgen Nachmittag |

Samstag		Sonntag	
10.00	angeln gehen	15.00	Katja besuchen
15.00	Golf spielen	**Montag**	
20.00	ins Kino gehen	9.30	zum Zahnarzt gehen

E.g. Morgen Vormittag geht Roland angeln.

A group of words and expressions describe how often something happens.

A Some useful expressions:

täglich *daily*	jeden Monat *every month*
jeden Morgen *every morning*	jedes Jahr *every year*
jeden Tag *every day*	
jedes Wochenende *every weekend*	

einmal *once*
zweimal *twice*
einmal in der Woche *once a week*
zweimal im Jahr *twice a year*
dreimal im Monat *three times a month*
morgens *in the mornings*
mittags *at midday*
nachmittags *in the afternoons*
abends *in the evenings*

Ich besuche meine Tante **zweimal im Jahr.**	*I visit my aunt twice a year.*
Ich stehe **morgens** um sieben Uhr auf.	*I get up at seven in the morning.*

These expressions (time adverbs) describe how often you do something, ranging from the least to the most frequently.

nie, niemals *never*	oft *often*
selten *seldom*	meistens *mostly*
ab und zu *now and again*	fast immer *nearly always*
manchmal *sometimes*	immer *always*

Ich gehe **oft** in die Stadt. *I often go to town.*
Ab und zu trinke ich Sekt. *I sometimes drink sekt.*

exercises

1 **Read the text and underline all the time expressions. Then write them down and translate them into English.**

Ich stehe jeden Morgen um 6.30 Uhr auf. Meistens dusche ich und zum Frühstück esse ich ein Brot mit Marmelade. Ich trinke manchmal Tee, aber nie Kaffee. Ich fahre fast immer mit der Straßenbahn zur Arbeit. Aber ab und zu gehe ich zu Fuß. Ich komme selten vor acht Uhr im Büro an. Mittags esse ich oft ein Brot im Büro.

2 **Can you put the time expression in the right place?**

E.g. Ich gehe ins Kino. (oft) → Ich gehe oft ins Kino.

a Ich trinke Kaffee. (manchmal)
b Steffi isst Eis. (oft)
c Andreas fährt mit dem Auto. (immer)
d Wir kaufen Obst auf dem Market. (jeden Samstag)

3 **Choose the most suitable time expression for each sentence.**

a Peter arbeitet _____ in der Firma.
b Er geht _____ in der Kantine essen.
c Um halb drei _____ fährt er nach Hause.
d _____ sieht er gern fern.

nachmittags
morgens
abends
mittags

Numbers like two, thirty-seven, one, ninety-nine, etc. are called cardinal numbers.

A Here are the cardinal numbers in German from one to twenty.

0	null		
1	eins	11	elf
2	zwei/zwo	12	zwölf
3	drei	13	dreizehn
4	vier	14	vierzehn
5	fünf	15	fünfzehn
6	sechs	16	sechzehn
7	sieben	17	siebzehn
8	acht	18	achtzehn
9	neun	19	neunzehn
10	zehn	20	zwanzig

Zwo is often used instead of **zwei** in spoken German to avoid confusion with **drei**; **sechzehn** drops the **s** in the middle, and **siebzehn** drops the **en**.

B

21	einundzwanzig	30	dreißig
22	zweiundzwanzig	40	vierzig
23	dreiundzwanzig	50	fünfzig
24	vierundzwanzig	60	sechzig
25	fünfundzwanzig	70	siebzig
26	sechsundzwanzig	80	achtzig
27	siebenundzwanzig	90	neunzig
28	achtundzwanzig		
29	neunundzwanzig		

Numbers from twenty upwards add **und** between the digits and are written as one word: neunundzwanzig 29.

Sechzig drops the **s** in the middle; **siebzig** drops the **en**; **dreißig** is spelt with **ß**.

C Telephone numbers are usually divided into groups of two:
14 45 60   vierzehn, fünfundvierzig, sechzig

The code is read as separate digits: 0793   null, sieben, neun, drei

exercises

1 Write out these sums as you would say them.

+ plus	− minus	× mal	÷ durch	= ist

E.g. 5 + 13 = ? fünf plus dreizehn ist achtzehn

a 7 + 2 = ?
b 11 + 5 = ?
c 13 − 1 = ?
d 3 × 5 = ?
e 32 ÷ 4 =
f 5 × 2 = ?
g 80 − 20 = ?

2 Find the missing numbers and write them in words.

E.g. ? × 7 = 35 → fünf

a 60 ÷ ? = 20
b 42 − ? = 31
c 24 ÷ 2 = ?
d ? + 25 = 30
e 72 − ? = 52

Numbers over a hundred are mostly written in figures; the amount on a cheque is written in both numbers and words.

A Hundreds, thousands, millions

(ein)hundert	100
hundertfünfzig	150
vierhundertsiebenundzwanzig	427
(ein)tausend	1.000
dreitausendsiebenhundertvierzig	3.740
eine Million(-en)	1.000.000
vier Millionen sechshunderttausenddreihundert	4.600.300
eine Milliarde(-n)	1.000.000.000

- There is usually no **und** after **hundert** and **tausend**.
- Thousands and millions in figures are separated either by a space or a full stop.
- Millions are written as separate words and take an **-en** in the plural.

B Years

achtzehnhundertsechzig	1860
neunzehnhundertneunundneunzig	1999

There is no *in* before the year in German. You either say just the year or **im Jahre ...** (*in the year ...*).

Ich bin neunzehnhundertachtundsechzig geboren. ⎫ *I was*
Ich bin im Jahre neunzehnhundertachtundsechzig ⎬ *born in*
  geboren. ⎭ *(the year) 1968.*

Er ist zweitausendzwei gestorben.	*He died in 2002.*
Ich war neunzehnhundertzweiundachtzig in Italien.	*I was in Italy in 1982.*

exercises

1 Find the matching pairs.

a 327	1	neunhundertsiebzehn
b 2 820	2	eine Million zweihundertfünfunddreißig-tausend
c 1 653 000	3	zweitausendfünfhundertvierundachtzig
d 194	4	hundertvierundneunzig
e 2 584	5	eine Million sechshundertdreiundfünfzig-tausend
f 1 235 000	6	zweitausendachthundertzwanzig
g 917	7	dreihundertsiebenundzwanzig

2 Write out the years as you would say them.

E.g. 1985 → neunzehnhundertfünfundachtzig

a 1996	d 2003
b 1963	e 1955
c 1890	

Erste (first), zwanzigste (twentieth), etc are known as ordinal numbers.

A To form the ordinal numbers from *first* to *nineteenth* add a -te ending to the cardinal number.

Erste, **dritte** and **siebte** are irregular forms

erste	*first*	elfte	*eleventh*
zweite	*second*	zwölfte	*twelfth*
dritte	*third*	dreizehnte	*thirteenth*
vierte	*fourth*	vierzehnte	*fourteenth*
fünfte	*fifth*	fünfzehnte	*fifteenth*
sechste	*sixth*	sechzehnte	*sixteenth*
siebte	*seventh*	siebzehnte	*seventeenth*
achte	*eighth*	achtzehnte	*eighteenth*
neunte	*ninth*	neunzehnte	*nineteenth*
zehnte	*tenth*		

B All numbers from *twentieth* upwards add an -ste ending.

zwanzig**ste**	*twentieth*
einundachtzig**ste**	*eighty-first*
hundert**ste**	*hundredth*
tausend**ste**	*thousandth*
million**ste**	*millionth*

C When you write an ordinal number in figures it has a full stop after it.

2. Klasse	*2nd class*

D Ordinal numbers are adjectives and add adjective endings when they come before a noun.

der dritt**e** Tag	*the third day*
die erst**en** Besucher	*the first visitors*
in dem zweit**en** Auto	*in the second car*

Mein Geburtstdatum ist der siebte vierte neunzehnhundertsiebzig.
My date of birth is 7/4/1970 (lit. the seventh of the fourth, i.e. seventh of April)

Heute ist der dritte sechste zweitausendzwei.
Today is the third of June (lit. the sixth) 2002.

exercise

1 Complete the sentences with an ordinal number.

E.g. das _____ Jahrhundert (*twenty-first century*) →
das einundzwanzigste Jahrhundert

a das _____ Jahrhundert (*twelfth century*)
b das _____ Baby (*first baby*)
c das _____ Mal (*second time*)
d der _____ Preis (*first prize*)
e die _____ Woche (*sixth week*)
f der _____ Tag (*third day*)
g die _____ Etage (*fourth floor*)
h der _____ Weltkrieg (*Second World War*)
i das _____ Auto (*millionth car*)
j die _____ Reise (*thousandth trip*)

How to say ³/₄, 40%, 15° etc. in German.

A To say *once*, *twice*, etc. in German, use the cardinal number with **mal** added.

ein**mal** *once*	x-**mal** *umpteen times*
zwei**mal** *twice*	

Ich besuche Martina **einmal** im Jahr.	*I visit Martina once a year*
Ich bin **x-mal** in Rom gewesen.	*I've been to Rome umpteen times.*

B To make fractions, add **-l** to the the end of the ordinal number.

⅓	ein Dritte**l**	*a third*
¼	ein Vierte**l**	*a quarter*
⅛	ein Achte**l**	*an eighth*
⅗	drei Fünfte**l**	*three-fifths*

The exception is **ein Halb** (*a half*).

1½	**anderthalb, eineinhalb**	*one and a half*
10½	**zehneinhalb**	*ten and a half*

Anderthalb is the more common expression for 1½ in everyday German.

C In German, decimals are written with a comma, not a point.

0,25	null **Komma** zwei fünf
1,9	eins **Komma** neun

D Percentages

2%	zwei **Prozent**
31,7%	einunddreißig Komma sieben **Prozent**

E Degrees

25°C	25 **Grad** (Celsius)	*25 degrees (Centigrade)*
–3°C	**minus** drei **Grad**	*minus three degrees*
+5°C	**plus** fünf **Grad**	*plus five degrees*

exercises

1 Look at this survey of favourite hobbies in Germany and write the results in full.

E.g. Achtundsechzig Prozent gehen schwimmen.

> schwimmen gehen 68%
> a Musik hören 42%
> b Gymnastik machen 33%
> c Rad fahren 24%
> d joggen gehen 23%
> e Tischtennis spielen 22 %
> f Fußball spielen 15%
> g Bücher lesen 10%
> h Zeitschriften lesen 8%
> i essen gehen 7%

2 Write the figures as you would say them.

E.g. 1,6 → eins Komma sechs

a 0,75

b 1,38

c 22°C

d ¼

e 5 ½

Prepositions plus article like **im** (in), **am** (on the) or **vom** (from the) are often used with the date in German.

A Here are the **Tage** *days* and **Monate** *months* in German.

Montag	Januar	Juli
Dienstag	Februar	August
Mittwoch	März	September
Donnerstag	April	Oktober
Freitag	Mai	November
Samstag/Sonnabend	Juni	Dezember
Sonntag		

Am Montag gehe ich zur Arbeit.	*I'm going to work on Monday.*
Karneval ist **im** Februar.	*Carnival is in February.*

B Ordinal numbers are used in dates.

Heute ist **der zwölfte April**. *It's the 12th of April today.*

C The ordinal number adds an **-n** (dative case) ending after the prepositions plus article **am** *on the* and **vom … bis zum …** *from … to …*

Ich bin **am siebten** Juni geboren.	*I was born on 7th June.*
vom neunten Juli **bis zum elften** August	*from 9th July to 11th August*

D After a day of the week, the date is in the accusative (**der** → **den**).

am Montag, **den achten** Februar *on Monday 8th February*

E In formal and informal letters, the date and the name of the place you are writing from appear at the top on the right. There is a comma after the place and a full stop after the number giving the date of the month. For example, Frankfurt, 18. Dezember 2002.

exercise

1 Here is your diary of important dates. Complete the sentences with the correct date.

E.g. *Am Donnerstag, den neunzehnten Dezember* fliege ich nach Amerika.

a _____ fahre ich nach München.
b _____ gehe ich zu Haralds und Astrids Hochzeit.
c _____ hat meine Mutter Geburtstag.
d _____ fliege ich nach Korsika.
e _____ fahre ich zu Marks Taufe.

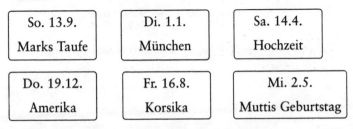

| So. 13.9. | Di. 1.1. | Sa. 14.4. |
| Marks Taufe | München | Hochzeit |

| Do. 19.12. | Fr. 16.8. | Mi. 2.5. |
| Amerika | Korsika | Muttis Geburtstag |

In Germany and Austria Euro, Kilo and Meter are the units of currency, weight and measurement.

A In Germany and Austria, the currency is **der Euro**. The coins are **Cent**. **100 Cent** make **1 Euro**. The words **Euro** and **Cent** do not change in the plural.

€0,20	zwanzig Cent
€5,40	fünf Euro vierzig
6 EUR	sechs Euro

In the German-speaking part of Switzerland, the currency is **Schweizer Franken** (Swiss francs). The small coins are called **Rappen** (100 *Rappen* = 1 *Franken*).

15,10 SF	fünfzehn Franken zehn
0,30 SF	dreißig Rappen

B **Gramm, Kilo**, etc. do not change in the plural. **Ein Pfund** (*a pound in weight*) is slightly more than a British pound.

1 g	ein Gramm
3 kg	drei Kilo(gramm)
1 Pfd.	ein Pfund (= ½ Kilo)
1 l	ein Liter

Zwei Kilo Kartoffeln kosten €2,10.	*Two kilos of potatoes cost 2 euros, 10 cents.*

In German there is no *of* after the expression of quantity.

C Measurements and distances

1 mm	ein Millimeter
2 cm	zwei Zentimeter
5 m	fünf Meter
8,20 m	acht Meter zwanzig
1 m²	ein Quadratmeter
6 m³	sechs Kubikmeter
10 km	10 Kilometer

exercises

1 How much does it cost?

E.g. 1 kg Äpfel/ €1,80M → Ein Kilo Äpfel kostet einen Euro achtzig.

a 2 kg Bananen/ €2,50
b 2 Pfd. Möhren/ €1,30

c 500g Butter/ €2,10
d 2 l Milch/ €1,40

2 Write out the measurements as you would say them.

E.g. zwei Zentimeter

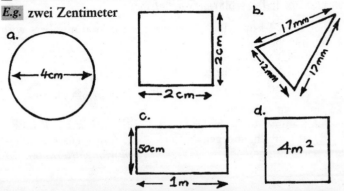

Both the 12-hour and (in more formal contexts) the 24-hour clock are used frequently German.

A The 12-hour clock

Es ist **ein Uhr**	*1 o'clock*
fünf nach eins	*1.05*
zehn nach eins	*1.10*
Viertel nach eins	*1.15*
zwanzig nach eins/zehn vor halb zwei	*1.20*
fünfundzwanzig nach eins/fünf vor halb zwei	*1.25*
halb zwei	*1.30*
fünfundzwanzig vor zwei/fünf nach halb zwei	*1.35*
zwanzig vor zwei/zehn nach halb zwei	*1.40*
Viertel vor zwei/drei Viertel zwei	*1.45*
zehn vor zwei	*1.50*
fünf vor zwei	*1.55*

Watch out for **halb** *half past* – in German you say *half to the next hour*: halb zwölf *half past eleven*.

B For the 24-hour clock, you use the cardinal numbers with **Uhr** after the hours.

14.07 Uhr: vierzehn Uhr sieben
00.15 Uhr: null Uhr fünfzehn
24.00 Uhr: vierundzwanzig Uhr

C Time expressions

Ich komme um sechs Uhr.	*I'll come at six o'clock.*
Es ist vier Uhr **morgens/**	*It's four o'clock in the*
nachmittags.	*morning/afternoon.*

Es ist zwölf Uhr **mittags**.   *It's noon/midday.*
Es ist zwölf Uhr **nachts/**   *It's midnight.*
Mitternacht/null Uhr.

Eine Stunde *one hour*, **eine Minute** *one minute* and **eine
Sekunde** *one second*. All add an **-n** in the plural.

Ich warte seit drei Stunden.   *I've been waiting for three
BUT   hours.*
Ich warte seit einer   *I've been waiting for
Dreiviertelstunde.   three-quarters of an hour.*

exercises

1 Say what time it is using the 12-hour clock.

E.g. 2:10 → Es ist zehn nach zwei.

a 4:45   d 6:05
b 7:00   e 9:20
c 5:10   f 8:50

2 Say when the trains arrive using the 24-hour clock.

E.g. Köln 14.02 → Der Zug aus
Köln kommt um vierzehn Uhr
zwei an.

Ankunft	Dortmund
Köln	14.02
a Gießen	07.14
b Leipzig	15. 27
c Oldenburg	23.59
d Würzburg	16.55
e Koblenz	18.22

This unit contains a list of the most common irregular, strong and mixed verbs. * indicates verbs which form their perfect and past perfect tenses with sein.

infinitive	present (er/sie/es)	simple past (er/sie/es)	past participle	meaning
backen	bäckt	backte	gebacken	*to bake*
beginnen	beginnt	begann	begonnen	*to begin*
bekommen	bekommt	bekam	bekommen	*to get, receive*
bieten	bietet	bot	geboten	*to offer*
bitten	bittet	bat	gebeten	*to ask*
bleiben	bleibt	blieb	*geblieben	*to stay*
brechen	bricht	brach	gebrochen	*to break*
bringen	bringt	brachte	gebracht	*to bring*
denken	denkt	dachte	gedacht	*to think*
dürfen	darf	durfte	gedurft	*to be allowed to*
empfehlen	empfiehlt	empfahl	empfohlen	*to recommend*
essen	isst	aß	gegessen	*to eat*
fahren	fährt	fuhr	*gefahren	*to go, to drive*
fallen	fällt	fiel	*gefallen	*to fall*
finden	findet	fand	gefunden	*to find*
fliegen	fliegt	flog	*geflogen	*to fly*
gebären	gebärt	gebar	*geboren	*to give birth to*
geben	gibt	gab	gegeben	*to give*
gefallen	gefällt	gefiel	gefallen	*to please*
gehen	geht	ging	*gegangen	*to go*
gelingen	gelingt	gelang	gelungen	*to succeed*
genießen	genießt	genoss	genossen	*to enjoy*
geschehen	geschieht	geschah	geschehen	*to happen*
gewinnen	gewinnt	gewann	gewonnen	*to win*
haben	hat	hatte	gehabt	*to have*
heißen	heißt	hieß	geheißen	*to be called*
helfen	hilft	half	geholfen	*to help*
kennen	kennt	kannte	gekannt	*to know (a person, a place)*
kommen	kommt	kam	gekommen	*to come*

können	kann	konnte	gekonnt	to be able to
lassen	lässt	ließ	gelassen	to leave, let, have done
laufen	läuft	lief	*gelaufen	to run
lesen	liest	las	gelesen	to read
liegen	liegt	lag	gelegen	to lie, be lying down
mögen	mag	mochte	gemocht	to like
müssen	muss	musste	gemusst	to have to
nehmen	nimmt	nahm	genommen	to take
reiten	reitet	ritt	*geritten	to ride
rufen	ruft	rief	gerufen	to call
schlafen	schläft	schlief	geschlafen	to sleep
schreiben	schreibt	schrieb	geschrieben	to write
schwimmen	schwimmt	schwamm	*geschwommen	to swim
sehen	sieht	sah	gesehen	to see
sein	ist	war	*gewesen	to be
singen	singt	sang	gesungen	to sing
sitzen	sitzt	saß	gesessen	to sit, be sitting
sollen	soll	sollte	gesollt	to be supposed to
sprechen	spricht	sprach	gesprochen	to speak
stehen	steht	stand	gestanden	to stand
steigen	steigt	stieg	*gestiegen	to climb
sterben	stirbt	starb	*gestorben	to die
tragen	trägt	trug	getragen	to carry, wear
treffen	trifft	traf	getroffen	to meet
trinken	trinkt	trank	getrunken	to drink
tun	tut	tat	getan	to do
vergessen	vergisst	vergaß	vergessen	to forget
verlassen	verlässt	verließ	verlassen	to leave
verlieren	verliert	verlor	verloren	to lose
verschwinden	verschwindet	verschwand	verschwunden	to disappear
waschen	wäscht	wusch	gewaschen	to wash
werden	wird	wurde	*geworden	to become
wissen	weiß	wusste	gewusst	to know (a fact)
wollen	will	wollte	gewollt	to want

A Present tense

Formation: stem of the verb + present-tense endings

The stem of regular verbs is formed by taking the -en off the infinitive.

singular		plural	
ich	-e	wir	-en
du	-st	ihr	-t
er/sie/es	-t	sie	-en
		Sie	-en

Ich spiele Tennis.   *I'm playing/I play tennis.*

B Perfect tense

Formation: present tense of **haben** or **sein** + past participle

Past participles:

- Weak verbs: **ge-** + **-t**
  ich habe gespielt   *I played, I have played*
  ich bin gewandert   *I hiked, I have hiked*

- Strong verbs: **ge-** + **-en**
  er hat gelesen   *he read, he has read*
  sie ist gegangen   *she went*

C Past perfect tense

Formation: simple past of **haben** or **sein** + past participle
  ich hatte gespielt   *I had played*
  er war gegangen   *he had gone*

D Simple past tense
Formation: stem of the verb + simple past endings

• Weak verbs

singular		plural	
ich	-te	wir	-ten
du	-test	ihr	-tet
er/sie/es	-te	sie	-ten
		Sie	-ten

• Strong verbs

singular		plural	
ich	–	wir	-en
du	-st	ihr	-et
er/sie/es	–	sie	-en
		Sie	-en

| ich kauf<u>te</u> | *I bought* |
| er f<u>u</u>hr | *he went, he travelled* |

E Future tense
Formation: present tense of **werden** + infinitive

| ich <u>werde</u> <u>kaufen</u> | *I will buy, I'm going to buy* |
| er <u>wird</u> <u>gehen</u> | *he'll go, he is going to go* |

F Passive
• Present passive
Formation: present tense of **werden** + past participle

| Das Fenster <u>wird</u> <u>repariert</u>. | *The window is being repaired.* |
| Die Häuser <u>werden</u> <u>gebaut</u>. | *The houses are being built.* |

A Case endings for **der, die, das, dieser, jeder, jener, welcher, mancher**

	masculine	feminine	neuter	plural
nom.	der	die	das	die
acc.	den	die	das	die
dat.	dem	der	dem	den
gen.	des	der	des	der

B Case endings for **ein, kein, mein, dein, sein, ihr, unser, euer, Ihr**

	masculine	feminine	neuter	plural
nom.	ein	eine	ein	keine
acc.	einen	eine	ein	keine
dat.	einem	einer	einem	keinen
gen.	eines	einer	eines	keiner

C Adjective endings after **der, dieser, jeder, mancher,** etc.

	masculine	feminine	neuter	plural
nom.	-e	-e	-e	-en
acc.	-en	-e	-e	-en
dat.	-en	-en	-en	-en
gen.	-en	-en	-en	-en

D Adjective endings after **ein, mein, kein,** etc.

	masculine	feminine	neuter	plural
nom.	-er	-e	-es	-en
acc.	-en	-e	-es	-en
dat.	-en	-en	-en	-en
gen.	-en	-en	-en	-en

E Adjective endings with no article.

	masculine	feminine	neuter	plural
nom.	-er	-e	-es	-e
acc.	-en	-e	-es	-e
dat.	-em	-er	-em	-en
gen.	-en	-er	-en	-er

F Summary of prepositions.

- **Accusative**: bis, durch, für, entlang (after noun), gegen, ohne, um.
- **Dative**: aus, bei, gegenüber, mit, nach, seit, von, zu.
- **Accusative or dative**: an, auf, hinter, in, neben, über, unter, vor, zwischen.
- **Genitive or dative**: statt, trotz, während, wegen.

G Summary of pronouns.

	nom.	acc.	dat.
I/me	ich	mich	mir
you	du	dich	dir
he/him/it	er	ihn	ihm
she/her/it	sie	sie	ihr
it	es	es	ihm
we/us	wir	uns	uns
you	ihr	euch	euch
they/them	sie	sie	ihnen
you	Sie	Sie	Ihnen

Unit 1: 1 a der **b** die **c** der **d** die **e** das **2 a** ein
b eine **c** ein **d** ein **e** eine **f** ein

Unit 2: 1 a das, das, das, <u>der</u> **b** das, das, <u>die</u>, das
c <u>das</u>, der, der, der **d** <u>der</u>, die, die, die **2 a** eine/*baker's*
b ein/*album* **c** ein/*cinema* **d** eine/*week* **e** ein/*radio*
f eine/*garage* **g** eine/*friendship* **h** ein/*centre* **i** eine/*religion*
j eine/*apartment*

Unit 3: 1 a der Wein, <u>das Bier</u>, der Whisky **b** der Junge,
der Mann, <u>das Baby</u> **c** das Küken, <u>der Bär</u>, das Lamm
d das Gold, das Silber, <u>die Bronze</u> **2 a** ein Elefant (*m.*) **b**
ein Arzt (*m.*) **c** ein Wein (*m.*) **d** ein Bier (*nt.*) **e** ein
Winter (*m.*) **f** ein Baby (*nt.*)

Unit 4: 1 a der Spanier **b** der Franzose **c** die Italienerin
d der Engländer **e** die Norwegerin **f** der Amerikaner
g die Griechin **2 a** die Ärztin **b** die Polizistin **c** die
Zahnärztin **d** die Köchin **e** die Architektin **f** die
Geschäftsfrau **g** die Lehrerin

Unit 5: 1 a der Stadtplan **b** das Telefonbuch **c** die
Kaffeemaschine **d** das Fußballstadion **e** die Teekanne
f der Goldfisch **g** die Tomatensuppe **h** das Schokoladeneis

Unit 6: 1 a die Leiter **b** der/das Keks **c** die Band
d das Golf **e** das Messer **f** das Pony

Unit 7: 1 a die Fische **b** die Pullover **c** die Brüder
d die Studenten **e** die Seen **f** die Monate **g** die Kuchen
2 a wohnen **b** arbeitet **c** sind **d** liegen

Unit 8: 1 a Schmidts **b** Kinder; Söhne **c** Autos
d Lehrerinnen **e** Söhne **2 a** die Mädchen **b** die
Italienerinnen **c** die Straßen **d** die Bäder **e** die Frauen
f die Sekretärinnen **g** die Hotels

Unit 9: 1 a 1 Er ist Portugiese. Sie ist Portugiesin **b** Er
ist Brite. Sie ist Britin **c** Er ist Schotte. Sie ist Schottin
d Er ist Österreicher. Sie ist Österreicherin **e** Er ist
Italiener. Sie ist Italienerin **f** Er ist Franzose. Sie ist
Französin **g** Er ist Spanier. Sie ist Spanierin **h** Er ist
Grieche. Sie ist Griechin **i** Er ist Afrikaner. Sie ist
Afrikanerin **j** Er ist Amerikaner. Sie ist Amerikanerin. **k**
Er ist Norweger. Sie ist Norwegerin. **l** Er ist Belgier. Sie ist
Belgierin.

Unit 10: 1 a Sie ist Friseurin. *She is a hairdresser.* **b** Er
ist Koch. *He is a chef.* **c** Sabine ist Krankenschwester.
Sabine is a nurse. **d** Herr Schmidt ist Geschäftsmann. *Mr
Schmidt is a businessman.* **2 a** Sie hat Zahnschmerzen.
b Er hat Bauchschmerzen. **c** Sie hat Rückenschmerzen.
d Er hat Halsschmerzen. **3 a** in dem/Im **b** – **c** Das
d – **e** – **f** –

Unit 11: 1 a Der Arzt **b** Der Hund **c** Die Frau
d Der Mann **e** Das Auto **f** Das Haus

Unit 12: 1 a Ich möchte einen Tisch kaufen. **b** Ich möchte
ein Sofa kaufen. **c** Ich möchte einen Herd kaufen. **d** Ich
möchte eine Lampe kaufen. **e** Ich möchte einen Stuhl kaufen.

f Ich möchte ein Bett kaufen. g Ich möchte eine Spülmaschine kaufen. h Ich möchte einen Kleiderschrank kaufen.

Unit 13: 1 a dem **b** dem **c** dem **d** der **e** dem
f den Kindern

Unit 14: 1 a Englands Königin heißt Elizabeth.
b Frankreichs Weine trinke ich gern. **c** Hamburgs Hafen ist an der Elbe. **d** Italiens Hauptstadt ist Rom. **e** Steven Spielbergs Filme sehe ich gern. **f** Beethovens Musik höre ich gern. **2 a** des Chefs **b** der **c** des Jahres **d** der **e** des Monats **f** der

Unit 15: 1 a Dieses **b** Welcher **c** Jedes **d** Manche **e** Welcher **f** Diese **g** Welcher

Unit 16: 1 a mein **b** seine **c** ihre **d** unser **e** deine
f euer **g** meine **h** Ihr **2 a** ihr **b** seine **c** ihre
d sein **e** mein

Unit 17: 1 a -en **b** -n **c** -n **d** -en **e** -n **f** -n **g** -en
h -en **i** -n **j** -en

Unit 18: 1 a ich spiele **b** du wohnst **c** er kommt/ macht/telefoniert/geht **d** sie kommt/macht/ telefoniert/geht **e** es regnet/kommt/macht/geht **f** studieren/besuchen/kaufen **g** ihr kommt/macht/telefoniert/geht **h** sie studieren/ besuchen/kaufen **i** Sie studieren/besuchen/ kaufen

Unit 19: 1 a spricht **b** schlafen **c** wäscht **d** gibt
e tragt **f** fährt **2 a** Kerstin fährt nach Paris. **b** Frau
Link arbeitet am Computer. **c** Monika isst im Restaurant.
d Du reist nächste Woche nach London. **e** Andreas isst
Apfelstrudel mit Sahne. **f** Du trägst einen blauen Pullover.
g Peter liest Zeitung.

Unit 20: 1 a hat **b** ist **c** sind **d** ist **e** Seid **f** hat
g Hast **h** habe **i** bist **j** sind **2 a** ist **b** sind
c hat **d** habe **e** hast **f** hat **g** haben

Unit 21: 1 a sei **b** lies **c** Esst **d** schlaf **e** fahr

Unit 22: 1 a 3 **b** 4 **c** 1 **d** 5 **e** 2 **2 a** hat …
gekocht **b** haben … geputzt **c** hat … gewohnt **d** haben
… gemacht

Unit 23: 1 a geschrieben **b** genommen **c** gegeben
d gesehen **e** gegessen **2 a** gefangen; *to catch*
b schlafen; *to sleep* **c** schneiden; geschnitten
d geschlossen; *to close* **e** getan; *to do* **f** lassen; gelassen

Unit 24: 1 a gewusst **b** studiert **c** gehabt **d** gekannt
2 a Wir haben eine Stunde gewartet. **b** Ich habe im Büro
gearbeitet. **c** Es hat den ganzen Tag geregnet. **d** Beate
hat mit Markus telefoniert. **e** Wir haben Glück gehabt.
f Georg hat in Berlin studiert. **g** Ich habe ihm geantwortet.

Unit 25: 1 a sind … gegangen **b** sind … gefahren
c bin … geschwommen **d** sind … geritten **e** sind …gesegelt

Unit 26: 1 a geschwommen; schwimmen (*to swim*)
b geritten; reiten (*to ride*) **c** geworden; werden (*to become*) **d** gewesen; sein (*to be*) **2 a** ist ... geboren
b ist ... gestorben **c** bin ... geblieben **d** Sind ... gewesen
e bist ... geworden

Unit 27: 1 Sie arbeiteten in dem Büro. Wir wohnten in
München. Ich spielte Tennis. Sie wartete zehn Minuten. Er
telefonierte mit seiner Frau. Du hörtest Musik. **2 a** Du
kauftest ein Auto. **b** Er kaufte eine Jacke. **c** Sie kauften
ein Buch. **d** Wir kauften Bananen. **e** Sie kauften einen
Fernseher. **f** Ihr kauftet Äpfel. **g** Sie kaufte eine Bluse.

Unit 28: 1 a ihr gabt **b** wir kamen/lasen **c** es ging
d du fuhrst **e** Sie lasen/kamen
2 a ging **b** traf **c** gingen
d gab **e** gingen **f** kam
g blieben

Unit 29: 1 a hatte **b** war **c** hatten **d** hatte **e** war
f warst **g** hatte

Unit 30: 1 a Man darf hier nicht parken. b Man darf hier nicht baden. c Man darf hier nicht fotografieren. d Man darf hier nicht essen. 2 a Ihr könnt ins Kino gehen. b Wir können zum Fußball gehen. c Sie können zum Weinfest gehen. d Du kannst ins Theater gehen. e Renate kann ins Jazzhaus gehen. f Lorenz kann ins Schwimmbad gehen.

Unit 31: 1 a muss; arbeiten b Willst; spielen c mag d soll; helfen e müssen; warten

Unit 32: 1 a Ich lasse die Fenster putzen. b Er lässt den Film entwickeln. c Ich lasse meine Augen untersuchen. d Frau Schmidt lässt das Zimmer streichen. e Ich lasse die Uhr reparieren. f Du lässt die Schuhe reparieren. g Ich lasse mir die Haare schneiden. 2 a Lass b lässt c Lass d lasse e lassen f Lass

Unit 33: 1 a wollte b sollten c mussten d musste e konnte f durfte

Unit 34: 1 a werden b werde c Wirst d wird e werden 2 a Er wird um 11.15 Uhr nach Rom fliegen. b Er wird um 12.00 Uhr Herrn Sachs treffen. c Er wird um 14.00 Uhr auf die Messe gehen. d Er wird um 18.00 Uhr mit Frau Antonio essen. e Er wird um 21.00 Uhr ins Theater gehen.

Unit 35: 1 a mich b sich c sich d sich e uns f dir 2 a Elke putzt sich die Zähne. b Sie zieht sich an. c Sie kämmt sich das Haar. d Sie schminkt sich.

Unit 36: 1 a 2 (regnet, gehe) **b** 4 (kommst, werden, spielen) **c** 1 (hat, macht) **d** 3 (bin, werde, koche)
2 a Wenn er zu spät kommt, verpasst er den Zug.
b Wenn ich Geld habe, werde ich eine Jacke kaufen.
b Wenn sie nach Hause kommt, werden wir Kuchen essen.

Unit 37: 1 a Wenn sie nach Freiburg kämen, würden sie ein Weinfest besuchen. **b** Wenn sie nach Freiburg kämen, würden sie in den Schwarzwald fahren. **c** Wenn sie nach Freiburg kämen, würden sie die Stadt besichtigen. **d** Wenn sie nach Freiburg kämen, würden sie den Markt besuchen.
e Wenn sie nach Freiburg kämen, würden sie ins Theater gehen.
2 a Wenn er Zeit hätte, würde er nach Frankreich fahren.
b Wenn ich Zeit hätte, würde ich nach China fahren.
c Wenn wir Zeit hätten, würden wir nach Dänemark fahren.
d Wenn Marion Zeit hätte, würde sie nach Indien fahren. **1**
3 Wenn ich Geld hätte, würde ich in Urlaub fahren.
b Wenn ich Geld hätte, würde ich eine Wohnung kaufen.
c Wenn ich Geld hätte, würde ich nach Australien fliegen.
d Wenn ich Geld hätte, würde ich ein Boot kaufen.

Unit 38: 1 a Ich möchte gern Rinderrouladen.
b Michael hätte gern Hühnerfrikassee. **c** Ich möchte gern gemischtes Eis. **d** Michael hätte gern Apfelstrudel.

Unit 39: 1 a Es gibt eine Lampe. **b** Es gibt einen Schreibtisch. **c** Es gibt einen Stuhl. **d** Es gibt ein Telefon.
e Es gibt einen Stift. **f** Es gibt eine Akte. **2 a** Es regnet.
b Es ist windig. **c** Es schneit. **d** Es ist nebelig.

Unit 40: 1 a Der Bus fährt um 11.15 Uhr ab. b Er fährt um 15.00 Uhr zurück. c Ich stehe um 6.30 Uhr auf. d Sie ruft um 14.00 Uhr an. e Der Bus kommt um 13.25 Uhr an. f Der Deutschkurs findet um 19.30 Uhr statt.

Unit 41: 1 a 5 b 7 c 1 d 8 e 2 f 3 g 6 h 4 2 a beginnt b verstehen c verkauft d übernachtet e empfehlen 3 a übernachten b bezahlt c versteht d übersetzt e bestellt

Unit 42: 1 a ein... b auf... c fern... d aus... 2 a umgezogen b eingeladen c ferngesehen d aufgestanden e mitgenommen

Unit 43: 1 a verloren b versprochen c übernachtet d verkauft e entschieden f bezahlt g bestellt 2 a Er hat €100,- verdient. b Der Film hat um 20 Uhr begonnen. c Wir haben ein Fahrrad verkauft. d Ich habe ein Paket bekommen. e Sie hat im Hotel übernachtet. f Hast du die Frage verstanden?

Unit 44: 1 a hatte b Hattest c war d hatte e haben f waren 2 a Jens war nach Paris gefahren. b Wir hatten Musik gehört. c Ich hatte meine Oma besucht. d Annette war in Rom geblieben. e Karl und Liane hatten im Büro gearbeitet.

Unit 45: 1 a – b – c zu d – e – f – g – h zu 2 a Er möchte nach Paris fahren, um den Eiffelturm zu besichtigen. b Wir möchten nach Washington fahren, um das Weiße Haus zu sehen. **c** Sie möchte nach Bayern fahren, um Schloss Neuschwanstein zu besichtigen. **d** Ich möchte nach China fahren, um die Große Mauer zu besichtigen. **e** Sie möchten nach Moskau fahren, um den Kreml zu sehen.

Unit 46: 1 a Er sagt, dass er ein Auto hat. **b** Sie sagen, dass sie in Mühlheim wohnen. **c** Er sagt, dass er zwanzig Jahre alt ist. **d** Sie sagt, dass sie einen Hund und zwei Katzen hat. **e** Sie sagen, dass sie samstags Fußball spielen. **f** Sie sagt, dass sie in einem Hotel im Schwarzwald arbeitet. **g** Sie sagt, dass sie einen Freund in Hamburg hat. **h** Er sagt, dass er gern Galerien in seiner Freizeit besucht.
2 a Er sagte, er sei für eine Woche in New York. **b** Er sagte, er sei im Hotel Atlantis. **c** Er sagte, er habe ein Fernsehinterview.

Unit 47: 1 a Bananen werden auf dem Markt verkauft. **b** Jacken werden im Modegeschäft verkauft. **c** Filme werden im Fotogeschäft verkauft. **d** CDs werden im Musikcenter verkauft.

Unit 48: 1 a wurde **b** wurden **c** wurde **d** wurden
2 a Der Bahnhof wurde 1902 gebaut. **b** Das Theater wurde 1893 gebaut. **c** Das Schloss wurde 1520 gebaut. **d** Der Palast wurde 1874 gebaut. **e** Das Museum wurde 1934 gebaut. **f** Die Kirche wurde 1487 gebaut. **g** Das Kloster wurde 1350 gebaut.

Unit 49: 1 a Er ist zu Hause. **b** Wir gehen in die Stadt.
c Sie arbeiten in Berlin. **d** Sie wartet vor dem Haus.
2 a Sie ist sehr alt. **b** Es ist in der Stadt. **c** Er schmeckt
gut. **d** Sie ist super.

Unit 50: 1 a 4 **b** 5 **c** 8 **d** 6/3 **e** 1 **f** 2 **g** 3/6
h 7 **2 a** Wir treffen sie vor dem Bahnhof. **b** Ich habe
ein Geschenk für ihn. **c** Ich muss ohne sie fahren. **d** Wann
möchtet ihr essen? **e** Hast du sie gesehen? **3 a** sie **b** sie
c ihn **d** es **e** ihn **f** sie **g** ihn

Unit 51: 1 a mir **b** ihm **c** du **d** uns **e** Sie **f** euch
g ihnen **h** es **2 a** ihr **b** ihm **c** ihnen **d** ihm
e euch **3 a** Es tut ihm Leid. **b** Es gefällt uns. **c** Wie
geht es dir? **d** Es tut ihnen Leid. **e** Es gefällt ihr. **f** Wie
geht es Ihnen?

Unit 52: 1 a Die Schwester, die in Aachen wohnt, ist
Studentin. **b** Der Onkel, der in Kiel wohnt, ist
Programmierer. **c** Die Tante, die in Hamm wohnt, ist
Hausfrau. **d** Das Kind, das in Kaiserslautern wohnt, ist
Schülerin. **e** Die Cousine, die in Hannover wohnt, ist
Friseurin. **f** Der Neffe, der in Hamburg wohnt, ist Grafiker.

Unit 53: 1 a Ich habe eine CD für meine Schwester.
b Ich habe Socken für meinen Vater. **c** Ich habe Blumen
für meine Mutter. **d** Ich habe ein Hemd für meinen Onkel.
e Ich habe einen Teddybär für meine Cousine. **2 a** Ich
fahre mit dem Schiff. **b** Ich fahre mit dem Zug. **c** Ich

fahre mit dem Fahrrad. **d** Ich fahre mit der Straßenbahn.
e Ich fahre mit dem Flugzeug.

Unit 54: 1 **a** 4 **b** 3 **c** 5 **d** 6 **e** 7 **f** 1 **g** 2
2 **a** bis **b** um **c** für

Unit 55: 1 **a** aus **b** bei **c** mit **d** seit **e** von **f** zu

Unit 56: 1 **a** die Bäckerei; der Bäckerei **b** den Bahnhof;
dem Bahnhof **c** das Kino; dem Kino **d** den Supermarkt;
dem Supermarkt **e** die Stadt; der Stadt **f** das Theater;
dem Theater **g** das Haus; dem Haus **h** den Garten; dem
Garten **i** die Küche; der Küche **j** das Wohnzimmer; dem
Wohnzimmer

Unit 57: 1 **a** dem **b** dem **c** der **d** dem; dem **e** dem
2 **a** die **b** die **c** dem **d** das **e** dem **f** dem; dem **g**
der **h** die

Unit 58: 1 **a** ans **b** vom **c** aufs **d** beim **e** im **f** zum
h ins 2 **a** Ich gehe zum Friseur. **b** Er geht zum Hotel.
c Wir gehen zur Post. **d** Du gehst zum Supermarkt.
e Sie geht zur Metzgerei. **f** Ich gehe zur Schule. **g** Sie
gehen zum Bahnhof.

Unit 59: 1 **a** 4 **b** 6 **c** 7 **d** 5 **e** 3 **f** 2 **g** 1
2 **a** Zu Weihnachten **b** in Urlaub **c** aufs Land **d** Zu
Ostern **e** Am Sonntag **f** nach Hause **g** zu Fuß
3 **a** vor einer Woche **b** Er ist zu Hause. **c** Sie fährt/geht
nach Hause. **d** Er fährt ins Ausland. **e** Ich bin auf
Dienstreise. **f** Wir gehen zu Fuß.

Unit 60: **1 a** für **b** um **c** über **d** in **e** auf **f** auf **g** an **2 a** auf **b** um **c** auf **d** um **e** an **f** auf **g** auf

Unit 61: **1 a** 9 **b** 10 **c** 1 **d** 7 **e** 6 **f** 3 **g** 8 **h** 2 **i** 4 **j** 5 **2 a** beginnen mit einer **b** mit dem ... sprechen **c** gratulieren ... zum **d** lädt ... zu einem ... ein **e** verabschiede ... von meinen

Unit 62: **1 a** groß; blond; groß; klein; ruhig; modern; freundlich; schlank; mittelgroß; warm; sonnig; lang; eng **2 a** Im Sommer ist es heiß und sonnig. **b** Im Herbst ist es kühl und regnerisch. **c** Im Winter ist es kalt und nebelig.

Unit 63: **1 a** billige **b** alte **c** frischen **d** italienische **e** jungen **f** neue **2 a** schwarze **b** neue **c** französischen **d** rote **e** alten **f** besten

Unit 64: **1 a** lange **b** kleiner **c** altes **d** neue **e** indisches **f** schlechte **g** linkes **h** schöner **2 a** einen braunen Hut **b** eine gelbe Jacke **c** einen grünen Rock **d** eine braune Handtasche

Unit 65: **1** neues Bett; runder brauner Tisch; alte Kommode; großer Kühlschrank **2 a** kurze, braune Haare. **b** schnelle Autos und große Hunde. **c** schlechtes Wetter **d** griechischen Käse und italienisches Eis **e** französischen Rotwein

Unit 66: **1 a** 8 **b** 6 **c** 7 **d** 5 **e** 3 **f** 1/2 **g** 1/2 **h** 4

Unit 67: 1 a später; 3 b älter; 6 c besser; 5 d langsamer; 1 e 10 stärker; f leiser; 7 g interessanter; 8 h ärmer; 4 i kürzer; 2 j größer; 9

Unit 68: 1 a beste b höchste c älteste d kleinste e längste f beste 2 a der kälteste Winter/der Winter ist am kältesten b die billigste Karte/die Karte ist am billigsten c die kleinste Katze/die Katze ist am kleinsten d der höchste Turm/der Turm ist am höchsten e das beste Restaurant/das Restaurant ist am besten f die jüngste Frau/die Frau ist am jüngsten g der kürzesteWeg/der Weg ist am kürzesten

Unit 69: 1 a Peter geht früher ins Bett als Konrad. b Peter singt besser als Konrad. c Konrad liest mehr als Peter.

Unit 70: 1 a Der Bus fährt um zehn Uhr nach Ulm. b Wir fliegen nächste Woche mit Julia nach Portugal. c Dirk war für zwei Wochen in Spanien. d Ich habe am Samstag im Park Tennis gespielt. 2 a ist … gefahren b kann … kaufen c wollen … besuchen d werde … arbeiten

Unit 71: 1 a Ich möchte nicht schwimmen gehen, sondern Golf spielen. b Ich trinke gern Kaffee und Tee mit Milch. c Ich wollte dich besuchen, aber ich musste zur Arbeit. d Willst du in die Kneipe gehen oder zu Hause bleiben? e Er fliegt im Winter nach Spanien, denn es ist dort wärmer. f Ich fahre entweder mit dem Zug oder mit dem Auto.

2 a aber b denn c entweder; oder d sondern 3 a
Wir möchten in Urlaub fahren, aber wir haben kein Geld.
b Er hat kein Auto sondern ein Motorrad. c Willst du
nach Portugal oder Spanien fahren?

Unit 72: 1 a 4 b 6 c 8 d 1 e 7 f 3 g 5 h 2
2 a Ich fahre nach Frankreich, weil ich Paris besuchen
möchte. b Ich fahre nach Deutschland, weil ich Berlin
besuchen möchte. c Ich fahre nach Griechenland, weil ich
Athen besuchen möchte.

Unit 73: 1 a 3 b 5 c 6 d 1 e 2 f 4 2 a Wo
b Warum c Was d Was für e Wohin f Wie viel

Unit 74: 1 a Wer b Wen c Wer d Wen e Wen
f Wer 2 a Wem b Wer c Wen d Wem e Wer
3 a Welche b Welcher c Welches d Welchen

Unit 75: 1 a Hast du Katrin gesehen? b Wann fahren wir
nach Basel? c Was hast du gestern gekauft? d Was
wollen wir am Samstag machen? e Was machst du
morgen? f Du hast Zeit, oder? g Warum kommt er so
spät? h Fahren wir nach Hamburg?

Unit 76: 1 a Oliver schwimmt nicht gern. b Oliver
fotografiert nicht gern. c Oliver geht nicht gern joggen.
d Oliver geht nicht gern ins Kino. e Oliver spielt nicht
gern Gitarre. f Oliver kocht nicht gern. 2 a Er ist nicht
gekommen. b Gestern war es nicht sonnig. c Sie geht
nicht zur Uni. d Morgen will ich nicht in die Kirche gehen.

e Ich gehe nicht gern spazieren. f Er ist nicht in der Stadt.
g Gehen Sie bitte nicht! h Wir wohnen nicht in Leipzig.

Unit 77: 1 a keine **b** kein **c** keine **d** kein **e** keinen
2 a Nein, danke. Ich möchte keine Schokolade. **b** Nein,
danke. Ich möchte keinen Kaffee. **c** Nein, danke. Ich
möchte kein Bier. **d** Nein, danke. Ich möchte keinen Wein.
e Nein, danke. Ich möchte kein Stück Kuchen. **f** Nein,
danke. Ich möchte keinen Orangensaft.

Unit 78: 1 a 7 **b** 4 **c** 1 **d** 9 **e** 3 **f** 10 **g** 8 **h** 2
i 6 **j** 5

Unit 79: 1 a 3 **b** 4 **c** 1 **d** 5 **e** 2 **2 a** Morgen
Nachmittag spielt Roland Golf. **b** Morgen Abend geht
Roland ins Kino. **c** Übermorgen besucht Roland Katja.
d Nächsten Montag geht Roland zum Zahnarzt.

Unit 80: 1 jeden Morgen (*every morning*); Meistens
(*mostly*); manchmal (*sometimes*); nie (*never*); fast
immer (*nearly always*); ab und zu (*now and again*); selten
(*seldom*); Mittags (*at midday*); oft (*often*) **2 a** Ich
trinke manchmal Kaffee. **b** Steffi isst oft Eis. **c** Andreas
fährt immer mit dem Auto. **d** Wir kaufen jeden Samstag
Obst auf dem Markt. **3 a** morgens **b** mittags
c nachmittags **d** Abends

Unit 81: 1 a sieben plus zwei ist neun **b** elf plus fünf ist sechzehn **c** dreizehn minus eins ist zwölf **d** drei mal fünf ist fünfzehn **e** zweiunddreißig durch vier ist acht **f** fünf mal zwei ist zehn **g** achtzig minus zwanzig ist sechzig. **2 a** drei **b** elf **c** zwölf **d** fünf **e** zwanzig

Unit 82: 1 a 7 **b** 6 **c** 5 **d** 4 **e** 3 **f** 2 **g** 1 **2 a** neunzehnhundertsechsundneunzig **b** neunzehnhundertdreiundsechzig **c** achtzehnhundertneunzig **d** zweitausend(und)drei **e** neunzehnhundertfünfundfünfzig

Unit 83: 1 a zwölfte **b** erste **c** zweite **d** erste **e** sechste **f** dritte **g** vierte **h** Zweite **i** millionste **j** tausendste

Unit 84: 1 a Zweiundvierzig Prozent hören Musik. **b** Dreiunddreißig Prozent machen Gymnastik. **c** Vierundzwanzig Prozent fahren Rad. **d** Dreiundzwanzig Prozent gehen joggen. **e** Zweiundzwanzig Prozent spielen Tischtennis. **f** Fünfzehn Prozent spielen Fußball. **g** Zehn Prozent lesen Bücher. **h** Acht Prozent lesen Zeitschriften. **i** Sieben Prozent gehen essen. **2 a** null Komma sieben fünf **b** eins Komma drei acht **c** zweiundzwanzig Grad **d** ein Viertel **e** fünfeinhalb

Unit 85: 1 a Am Dienstag, den ersten Januar **b** Am Samstag, den vierzehnten April **c** Am Mittwoch, den zweiten Mai **d** Am Freitag, den sechzehnten August **e** Am Sonntag, den dreiundzwanzigsten September

Unit 86: 1 a Zwei Kilo Bananen kosten zwei Euro fünfzig. b Zwei Pfund Möhren kosten einen Euro dreißig. c Fünfhundert Gramm Butter kosten zwei Euro zehn. d Zwei Liter Milch kosten einen Euro vierzig. 2 a vier Zentimeter b siebzehn Millimeter, zwölf Millimeter c ein Meter, fünfzig Zentimeter d vier Quadratmeter

Unit 87: 1 a Es ist Viertel vor fünf/drei Viertel fünf. b Es ist sieben Uhr. c Es ist zehn nach fünf. d Es ist fünf nach sechs e Es ist zwanzig nach neun/zehn vor halb zehn. f Es ist zehn vor neun. 2 a Der Zug aus Gießen kommt um sieben Uhr vierzehn an. b Der Zug aus Leipzig kommt um fünfzehn Uhr siebenundzwanzig an. c Der Zug aus Oldenburg kommt um dreiundzwanzig Uhr neunundfünfzig an. d Der Zug aus Würzburg kommt um sechzehn Uhr fünfundfünfzig an. e Der Zug aus Koblenz kommt um achtzehn Uhr zweiundzwanzig an.

Exercise 1 (Unit 5)

Name each place by finding the correct pair of nouns and making a compound noun.

die Reise/das Büro   der Bus/der Bahnhof
~~der Rat/das Haus~~   der Schuh/das Geschäft
die Kinder/der Spielplatz   die Halle/das Bad

E.g.

das Rathaus

a

b

c

d

e

Exercise 2 (Unit 7)

Write these nouns in the plural.

E.g. der Mann → die Männer

a der Finger _____

b der Tag _____

c der Sohn_____

d der Hund _____

e der Mensch _____

f der Schuh _____

Exercise 3 (Unit 8)

Label the parts of the body. Put each noun into the plural.

| der Finger | ~~der Fuß~~ | die Hand | das Auge | das Bein |

die Füße

Exercise 4 (Unit 11)

Put in ein, eine or ein in the nominative case. The subject is marked in bold and its gender is given in brackets.

E.g. _____ **Kiste** (f.) Wasser kostet €6,–. →
Eine **Kiste** Wasser kostet €6,–.

a _____ **Packung** (f.) Kekse kostet €1,99.

b _____ **Becher** (m.) Jogurt kostet €0,40.

c _____ **Dose** (f.) Erbsen kostet €0,60.

d _____ **Glas** (nt.) Marmelade kostet €1,99.

e _____ **Flasche** (f.) Wein kostet €3,50.

Exercise 5 (Unit 11)

Put der, die or das into the the sentence. The gender of the subject is given in brackets.

E.g. _____ **Zug** (m.) fährt nach Paris. →
Der **Zug** fährt nach Paris.

a _____ **Bus** (m.) aus Hameln kommt um halb elf.

b _____ **Bäckerei** (f.) ist in der Poststraße.

c _____ **Haus** (nt.) hat acht Zimmer.

d Gestern kam _____ **Brief** (m.) von meiner Freundin.

e _____ **Frau** (f.) hat eine Tochter.

Exercise 6 (Unit 12)

Complete the sentences with the accusative form of der/die/das or ein/eine/ein. The first letter of the article is given.

E.g. Wir suchen e_____ Campingplatz (*m.*). →
Wir suchen *einen* Campingplatz.

a Wir möchten e_____ Doppelzimmer (*nt.*) reservieren.

b   Er braucht e_____ neue Jacke (*f.*).

c Kennst du d_____ Restaurant (*nt.*) in der Salzstraße?

d Ich habe e_____ Idee (*f.*)!

e Hast du d_____ Film (*m.*) schon gesehen?

f Sie möchte e_____ Glas (*nt.*) Wein.

g Er war e_____ Woche (*f.*) in London.

h Ich war für e_____ Tag (*m.*) in Trier.

Exercise 7 (Unit 13)

Underline the indirect object in these sentences.

E.g. Sandra gibt <u>dem Mann</u> eine Karte.

a Er bringt dem Mädchen ein Eis.

b Ich danke der Dame für die Information.

c Meine Frau erzählt dem Jungen von unserem Urlaub.

d Zeigen Sie dem Kunden das neue Auto.

Exercise 8 (Unit 13)

Build sentences from the table. Use the pictures to help you.

E.g. **Ich schenke dem Baby einen Teddy.**

a Ich schenke	dem Patienten	Blumen.
b Alex schickt	dem Kunden	**einen Teddy.**
c Die Krankenschwester gibt	**dem Baby**	eine Tablette.
d Der Mechaniker zeigt	einer Freundin	das Auto

Exercise 9 (Unit 14)

Put the expressions in bold into the genitive case.

E.g. das Auto **von dem Mann**. (m.) →
das Auto **des Mannes**.

a der Manager **von der Bank**. (*f.*)
b das Büro **von dem Manager**. (*m.*)
c der Mantel **von der Frau**. (*f.*)
d der Bruder **von dem Mann**. (*m.*)

Exercise 10 (Unit 16)

What have these people lost? Write sentences with the correct possessive form. Use the accusative case.

E.g. Thomas, ein Regenschirm (*m.*) →
Thomas hat *seinen* Regenschirm verloren.

a Marion, ein Portemonnaie (*nt.*)
b Anja, ein Stift (*m.*)
c Lars, eine Katze (*f.*)
d Liane, ein Schal (*m.*)
e Torsten, eine Mütze (*f.*)

Exercise 11 (Unit 17)

Add an ending to the noun where necessary.

E.g. Der Junge_____ ist zu Hause. →
Der Junge ist zu Hause. (nom.)
Ich kenne den Kunde_____. →
Ich kenne **den Kunden**. (acc.)

a Der Kollege_____ ist freundlich.

b Ich kenne den Architekt_____ .

c Der Elefant_____ ist sehr groß.

d Ich habe den Affe_____ im Zoo gesehen.

e Der Nachbar_____ ist in Urlaub.

f Kennst du den Junge_____ ?

Exercise 12 (Unit 18)

Complete the sentences with the correct form of the verb in brackets.

E.g. Er _____ mit seiner Mutter. (telefonieren) →
Er telefoniert mit seiner Mutter.

a Wann _____ ihr? (kommen)

b Wohin _____ du am Samstag? (gehen)

c Das Mädchen _____ zu Hause. (bleiben)

d Was _____ du heute Nachmittag ? (machen)

e Er _____ Markus. (besuchen)

f Wo _____ ihr? (studieren)

g Heike und Robert _____ gern Tennis. (spielen)

h Dirk _____ in München. (wohnen)

Exercise 13 (Unit 20)

Translate the following sentences into German.

E.g. Are you thirsty? → Hast du Durst?

a He is a doctor.
b I've got blonde hair.
c They are in London.
d We're hungry.
e She is frightened.
f I have a flat.

Exercise 14 (Unit 20)

Make command forms.

E.g. du/nach Hause gehen → *Geh* nach Hause!

a ihr/am Wochenende kommen
b Sie/das Buch lesen
c du/ein Eis kaufen
d ihr/im Garten spielen
e ihr/ruhig sein

Exercise 15 (Unit 20)

What sports did they play?

E.g. Simone/Golf → Simone *hat* Golf *gespielt*.

a Klaus und Heiko/Tennis
b Tobias/Handball
c Ulrike und Max/Badminton
d Ruth/Hockey

Exercise 16 (Unit 22)

Write sentences in the perfect to say what these people did yesterday.

E.g. Wir/Musik/hören → Wir *haben* Musik *gehört.*

a Steffi/ein Kleid/kaufen
b Tanja/in der Disko/tanzen
c Er/Klavier/spielen
d Ihr/Fitnesstraining/machen
e Du/Hausaufgaben/machen
f Anja und Silke/Eis/bestellen
g Ich/Schuhe/kaufen

Exercise 17 (Unit 23)

Complete each sentence with the correct form of the verb haben and a suitable past participle from the box.

getroffen   gegessen   gelesen   gefunden   getrunken   ~~gesehen~~

E.g. Ich _____ einen Krimi im Fernsehen _____ . →
Ich habe einen Krimi im Fernsehen gesehen.

a Rainer _____ gestern ein Buch _____ .
b Daniel _____ einen Freund im Bistro _____ .
c _____ du deinen Schlüssel _____ ?
d Zum Abendessen _____ wir Steak mit Pommes _____ und
Rotwein _____ .

Exercise 18 (Unit 25)

Complete the sentences with the correct form of the verb sein.

E.g. Ich _____ um neun Uhr gekommen. →
Ich *bin* um neun Uhr gekommen.

a Wir_____ letzten Sommer nach Amerika geflogen.

b Mara _____ nach Hause gelaufen.

c Sie_____ zum Supermarkt gefahren.

d Alex _____ gestern Abend in die Disko gegangen.

e Warum _____ ihr nicht gekommen?

f Ich _____ in Österreich in den Bergen gewandert.

g _____ ihr gestern in die neue Kneipe gegangen?

Exercise 19 (Unit 26)

Ask questions in the perfect tense using sein + past participle.

E.g. Wann/Sie/zu Hause/sein →
Wann sind Sie zu Hause gewesen?

a Wann/Sie/auf der Messe/sein

b Warum/die Fähre/sinken

c Was/mit Ingo/passieren

d Warum/du/gestern/verschwinden

Exercise 20 (Unit 26)

Sein or haben? Underline the correct verb.

E.g. Wir <u>sind</u>/haben nach Frankreich gefahren.

a Ich habe/bin nach Italien gefahren.

b Sie hat/ist das Motorrad gefahren.

c Er hat/ist geritten.
d Ich bin/habe im Atlantik die Yacht gesegelt.

Exercise 21 (Unit 28)

Write sentences in the simple past.

E.g. Ich/finden/ €100 auf der Straße →
Ich fand €100 auf der Straße.

a Wir/essen/Eis
b Erika/fliegen/nach Amerika
c Sie (*They*)/fahren/mit dem Bus
d Er/trinken/Tee
e Du/schreiben/einen Brief

Exercise 22 (Unit 29)

Use the simple past to say where these people were in the summer.

E.g. Wir/Spanien → Wir waren in Spanien.

a Angelika/Frankreich
b Du/Italien
c Andrea und Boris/England
d Johannes/Deutschland
e Ich/Amerika.

Exercise 23 (Unit 29)

What is the simple past form of these verbs?

E.g. bringen (ich) → ich brachte

a wissen (er)

b denken (ich)

c anfangen (wir)

d werden (ich)

Exercise 24 (Unit 30)

What can you do in these cities this week?

E.g. Köln/dieAusstellung/besuchen →
    Du kannst die Austellung in Köln besuchen.

a Mannheim/das Museum/besuchen

b Düsseldorf/zum Fußballspiel/gehen

c Hamburg/das Theater/besuchen

d München/zum Oktoberfest/gehen

e Stuttgart/die Messe/besuchen

f Basel/zur Modenschau/gehen

Exercise 25 (Unit 31)

Add the correct form of the verbs.

E.g. Wir _____ zum Zahnarzt _____ . (sollen/gehen) →
    Wir sollen zum Zahnarzt gehen.

a Er _____ samstags _____ . (müssen/arbeiten)

b _____ du Karten _____ ? (wollen/spielen)

c Ich _____ Krimis. (mögen)

d Alexander _____ uns im Garten _____ . (sollen/helfen)

e Die Kinder _____ nicht _____ . (müssen/warten)

Exercise 26 (Unit 33)

Make sentences using the simple past.

E.g. Er/im Wald/spazieren/wollen →
     Er wollte im Wald spazieren.

a Ich/ins Konzert/gehen/wollen

b Frau Kramer/im Büro/arbeiten/sollen

c Sie (*They*)/zu Hause/bleiben/können

d Wir/meine Tante/besuchen/wollen

e Er/zur Bank/gehen/müssen

Exercise 27 (Unit 35)

Write sentences describing what they are putting on today.

E.g. Miriam/ein Kleid → Miriam zieht sich ein Kleid an.

a Erika/eine Jeans

b ich/ein Hemd

c Elke/eine Jacke

d Max/Schuhe

Exercise 28 (Unit 36)

Make sentences

E.g. kalt/ich/Ski fahren/gehen →

Wenn es morgen kalt ist, gehe ich Ski fahren.

a sonnig/er/schwimmen/gehen

b windig/wir/nicht spazieren/gehen

c regnet/Mara/Musik/hören

d schön/ich/reiten/gehen

e schneit/Bernd und Klaus/ins Kino/gehen

f nebelig/Tina/zu Hause/bleiben

Exercise 29 (Unit 38)

Put a verb from the box into each sentence to make a polite request.

möchtest	hätte gern	möchte	würden	könnten

a Ich _____ einen Tee.

b _____ Sie mir bitte helfen?

c _____ Sie bitte das Fenster aufmachen?

d _____ du ein Stück Kuchen?

e Ich _____ gern einen Kaffee.

Exercise 30 (Unit 38)

Make polite requests

E.g. werden/die Speisekarte geben →
Würden Sie mir die Speisekarte geben?

a werden/das Fenster schließen
b können/mir das Wort erklären
c werden/mir ein Bier bringen
d können/einen Moment warten

Exercise 31 (Unit 39)

Make sentences from the words in the box which correspond to the translations.

| Leid | ~~ihm~~ | egal | ~~gefällt~~ | gut | ist | weh |
| | mir | ihr | tut | kalt | geht | mir |

E.g. He likes it. Es … → Es gefällt ihm.

a *She doesn't mind.* Es …
b *It hurts (me).* Es …
c *It's cold.* Es …
d *I'm sorry.* Es …

Exercise 32 (Unit 40)

Match a prefix to each of the verbs and give the English
meaning.

| auf | statt | fern | um | an | ab | zurück |

E.g. _____steigen → umsteigen (*to change (trains)*)

a _____kommen

b _____sehen

c _____stehen

d _____finden

e _____holen

f _____fahren

Exercise 33 (Unit 40)

Make sentences using the information given.

E.g. Dieter/um sieben Uhr/aufstehen →
Dieter steht um sieben Uhr auf.

a Wir/in Düsseldorf/umsteigen

b Er/nach Hameln/zurückfahren

c Ich/in der Burgstraße/aussteigen

d Die Messe/in Köln/stattfinden.

e Ich/dich morgen Abend/anrufen

Exercise 34 (Unit 42)

Complete the sentences with the correct form of haben or sein.

E.g. Ich _____ Claudia abgeholt. →

Ich habe Claudia abgeholt.

a Er _____ Annette zu seiner Geburtstagsparty eingeladen.

b Evi _____ um 19.00 Uhr angekommen.

c Wir _____ in den Zug eingestiegen.

d Ich _____ mein Zimmer aufgeräumt.

e Meine Frau _____ gestern um 6.30 Uhr zurückgefahren.

Exercise 35 (Unit 47)

Where are these goods produced? Write sentences using the present passive.

E.g. Swatch Uhren /in der Schweiz →

Swatch Uhren werden in der Schweiz produziert.

a Mercedes/in Deutschland

b Computer/in Japan

c Fernseher/in den USA

d Motorräder/in England

e Ferraris/in Italien

f Jeans/in Taiwan

g Peugeots/in Frankreich

Exercise 36 (Unit 52)

What did you buy? Formulate sentences using relative pronouns referring to the object in the accusative case.

E.g. das Auto/rot → Das Auto, das ich gekauft habe, ist rot.

a der Pullover/grün
b das Hemd/gestreift.
c die Bluse/schwarz
d der Mantel/braun
e die Schuhe/blau
f die Hose (*sing.*)/schwarz

Exercise 37 (Unit 56)

Describe the pictures.

E.g. Die Katze ist hinter dem Stuhl.

a

b

c    d

Exercise 38 (Unit 62)

Use these different adjectives to describe each person.

traurig	groß	hübsch	klein	gut gebaut
	freundlich		schlank	

a   b

a Der Mann ist …
b Die Frau ist … und der Mann ist …

Exercise 39 (Unit 64)

Complete each sentence with the adjective and add the correct ending (nominative, accusative or dative case).

E.g. Ich habe ein _____ Problem. ((*nt.*) groß) →
Ich habe ein *großes* Problem.

a Ich habe einen _____ Computer. ((*m.*) neu)
b Moni ist eine _____ Studentin. ((*f.*) intelligent)
c Wir haben ein _____ Haus am See. ((*nt.*) klein)
d Jan geht mit einer _____ Freundin ins Kino. ((*f.*) gut)
e Ich fahre mit einem _____ Fahrrad zur Schule. ((*nt.*) alt)

Exercise 40 (Unit 65)

Complete the newspaper advertisement by adding the correct adjective endings.

> **Wohnungen/Häuser**
> Schön_____ , hell_____ 2 Zi. Wohnung (*f.*), sehr
> ruhig_____ Lage (*f.*), separat_____ WC (*nt.*),
> groß_____ Küche (*f.*), neu_____ Bad (*nt.*), klein_____
> Keller (*m.*) 75m², €500,-. Tel. 60 67 89

Exercise 41 (Unit 66)

Translate these expressions into German.
a Good evening.
b Happy New Year.

c Happy Birthday
d Good night.
e Have a nice weekend.
f Enjoy your meal.
g Good day.
h Thank you very much.

Exercise 42 (Unit 66)

How would you close letters which open with these expressions?

E.g. Sehr geehrter Herr Thoma → Mit freundlichen Grüßen

a Lieber Markus
b Sehr geehrte Damen und Herren
c Liebe Martina
d Sehr geehrte Frau Feldmann

Exercise 43 (Unit 67)

Match each comparative to its English meaning.

a kälter   1 *warmer*
b jünger   2 *higher*
c länger   3 *colder*
d wärmer   4 *weaker*
e härter   5 *younger*
f höher   6 *longer*
g schwächer   7 *harder*

Exercise 44 (Unit 68)

Write two sentences about each pair making comparisons.

> *E.g.* die USA/Deutschland/groß →
> Die USA sind größer als Deutschland.
> Deutschland ist nicht so groß wie die USA.

a der Rhein/die Themse/lang
b eine Maus/eine Katze/klein
c ein Porsche/ein Mini/schnell
d der Everest/Ben Nevis/hoch
e England/Australien/kälter
f Indien/Amerika/arm
g Mein Bruder/ich/alt

Exercise 45 (Unit 69)

Complete the sentences with a verb and the superlative adverbs.

> *E.g.* Dirk läuft langsamer als Stefan. →
> Gerd *läuft am langsamsten.*

a Jens fährt schneller als Klaus. Frank ...
b Steffi arbeitet besser als Lena. Karola ...
c Rolf kommt später als Georg. Bernhard ...
d Jan wartet länger als Franziska. Alicia ...
e Ich koche schlechter als Marion. Doris ...

Exercise 46 (Unit 72)

Combine the two sentences with the subordinating conjunction to make one new sentence.

E.g. Ich arbeite am Computer. Ich bin müde. (obwohl) →
Ich arbeite am Computer, obwohl ich müde bin.

a Er hört jeden Tag Radio. Er frühstückt. (während)
b Ich gehe zum Arzt. Ich bin krank. (wenn)
c Er liest Zeitung. Er ist zu Hause. (sobald)
d Wir lernen Deutsch. Wir fahren nächstes Jahr nach Deutschland. (weil)

Exercise 47 (Unit 81)

Write out these telephone numbers.

E.g. 79 04 25 → Meine Telefonnummer ist neunundsiebzig null vier fünfundzwanzig.

a 44 23 30
b 11 47 56
c 81 09 62
d 93 12 75

Exercise 48 (Unit 82)

Look at the statistics for the average number of kilometres driven per inhabitant per year. Write out the numbers as you would say them.

E.g. Kanada 8 800 → achttausendachthundert

a USA 14 100
b Australien 9 300
c Großbritannien 7 000
d Deutschland 6 600
e Spanien 2 600
f Frankreich 3 100
g Italien 4 500

Exercise 49 (Unit 83)

Write out these dates in words.

E.g. Heute ist der (1.2.1999) → Heute ist der erste zweite
    neunzehnhundertneunundneunzig.

a Heute ist der (7.8.).
b Gestern war der (27.11.).
c Morgen ist der (31.7.).
d Der (14.) ist ein Montag.
e Marions Geburtstag ist der (26.5.1959).
f Jans Geburtsdatum ist der (3.9.1966).
g Was ist Ihr Geburtsdatum? Mein Geburtsdatum ist der ...
h Der Wievielte ist heute? Heute ist der ...

Exercise 50 (Unit 84)

Complete the sentences with *once*, *twice* et..

E.g. Ich putze mein Auto _____ im Jahr. (5x) →
    Ich putze mein Auto *fünfmal* im Jahr.

a Wir fahren in Urlaub _____ im Jahr. (2x)

b Er liest die Zeitung _____ in der Woche. (4x)

c Sie geht _____ im Monat ins Kino. (3x)

d Ich sehe _____ in der Woche fern. (5x)

e Ich habe _____ angerufen. (1x)

Exercise 51 (Unit 85)

What's the date today?

E.g. 3.4. → Heute ist der dritte April.

a 6.7.

b 12.1.

c 1.5.

d 3.10.

Exercise 52 (Unit 85)

Complete the sentences with from ... to ... . Write the dates in words.

E.g. 2.4. – 6.4.   Lucy hat _____ Urlaub. →

Lucy hat vom zweiten bis zum sechsten April Urlaub.

a 1.3.–10.3.   Markus hat _____ Urlaub.

b 19.7.–25.7.   Ich möchte ein Doppelzimmer _____ reservieren.

c 30.11.–3.12.   Ich bin _____ auf Geschäftsreise in Hamburg.

Exercise 53 (Unit 87)

Write out these stopwatch times in words.

E.g. 2.15.02 → zwei Stunden fünfzehn Minuten und zwei Sekunden

a 7.29.08

b 4.16.38

c 3.44.12

Exercise 1 (Unit 5): a das Hallenbad b der Kinderspielplatz c der Busbahnhof d das Reisebüro e das Schuhgeschäft

Exercise 2 (Unit 7): a die Finger b die Tage c die Söhne d die Hunde e die Menschen f die Schuhe

Exercise 3 (Unit 8): a die Augen b die Hände c die Finger d die Beine

Exercise 4 (Unit 11): a Eine b Ein c Eine d Ein e Eine

Exercise 5 (Unit 11): a Der b Die c Das d der e Die

Exercise 6 (Unit 12): a ein b eine c das d eine e den f ein g eine h einen

Exercise 7 (Unit 13): a dem Mädchen b der Dame c dem Jungen d dem Kunden

Exercise 8 (Unit 13): a Ich schenke dem Baby einen Teddy. b Alex schickt einer Freundin Blumen. c Die Krankenschwester gibt dem Patienten eine Tablette. d Der Mechaniker zeigt dem Kunden das Auto.

Exercise 9 (Unit 14): a der Manager der Bank b das Büro des Managers c der Mantel der Frau d der Bruder des Mannes

Exercise 10 (Unit 16): a Marion hat ihr Portemonnaie verloren. **b** Anja hat ihren Stift verloren. **c** Lars hat seine Katze verloren. **d** Liane hat ihren Schal verloren. **e** Torsten hat seine Mütze verloren.

Exercise 11 (Unit 17): a Kollege **b** Architekten **c** Elefant **d** Affen **e** Nachbar **f** Jungen

Exercise 12 (Unit 18): a kommt **b** gehst **c** bleibt **d** machst **e** besucht **f** studiert **g** spielen **h** wohnt

Exercise 13 (Unit 20): a Er ist Arzt. **b** Ich habe blondes Haar. **c** Sie sind in London. **d** Wir haben Hunger. **e** Sie hat Angst. **f** Ich habe eine Wohnung.

Exercise 14 (Unit 21): a Kommt am Wochenende! **b** Lesen Sie das Buch! **c** Kauf ein Eis! **d** Spielt im Garten! **e** Seid ruhig!

Exercise 15 (Unit 22): a Klaus und Heiko haben Tennis gespielt. **b** Tobias hat Handball gespielt. **c** Ulrike und Max haben Badminton gespielt. **d** Ruth hat Hockey gespielt.

Exercise 16 (Unit 22): a Steffi hat ein Kleid gekauft. **b** Tanja hat in der Disko getanzt. **c** Er hat Klavier gespielt. **d** Ihr habt Fitnesstraining gemacht. **e** Du hast Hausaufgaben gemacht. **f** Anja and Silke haben Eis bestellt. **g** Ich habe Schuhe gekauft.

Exercise 17 (Unit 23): a hat … gelesen **b** hat … getroffen **c** Hast … gefunden **d** haben … gegessen/getrunken

Exercise 18 (Unit 25): a sind **b** ist **c** ist **d** ist **e** seid **f** bin **g** Seid

Exercise 19 (Unit 26): a Wann sind Sie auf der Messe gewesen? **b** Warum ist die Fähre gesunken? **c** Was ist mit Ingo passiert? **d** Warum bist du gestern verschwunden?

Exercise 20 (Unit 26): a bin **b** hat **c** ist **d** habe

Exercise 21 (Unit 28): a Wir aßen Eis. **b** Erika flog nach Amerika. **c** Sie fuhren mit dem Bus. **d** Er trank Tee. **e** Du schriebst einen Brief.

Exercise 22 (Unit 29): a Angelika war in Frankreich. **b** Du warst in Italien. **c** Andrea und Boris waren in England. **d** Johannes war in Deutschland. **e** Ich war in Amerika.

Exercise 23 (Unit 29): a wusste **b** dachte **c** fingen an **d** wurde

Exercise 24 (Unit 30): a Du kannst das Museum in Mannheim besuchen. **b** Du kannst zum Filmfest in Düsseldorf fahren. **c** Du kannst das Theater in Hamburg besuchen. **d** Du kannst auf das Oktoberfest in München gehen. **e** Du kannst die Messe in Stuttgart besuchen. **f** Du kannst zur Modenschau in Basel gehen.

Exercise 25 (Unit 31): a muss; arbeiten **b** Willst; spielen
c mag **d** soll; helfen **e** müssen; werken

Exercise 26 (Unit 33): a Ich wollte ins Konzert gehen.
b Frau Kramer sollte im Büro arbeiten. **c** Sie konnten zu
Hause bleiben. **d** Wir wollten meine Tante besuchen.
e Er musste zur Bank gehen.

Exercise 27 (Unit 35): a Erika zieht sich eine Jeans an.
b Ich ziehe mir ein Hemd an. **c** Elke zieht sich eine Jacke
an. **d** Max zieht sich Schuhe an.

Exercise 28 (Unit 36): a Wenn es morgen sonnig ist, geht er
schwimmen. **b** Wenn es morgen windig ist, gehen wir
nicht spazieren. **c** Wenn es morgen regnet, hört Mara
Musik. **d** Wenn es morgen schön ist, gehe ich reiten.
e Wenn es morgen schneit, gehen Bernd und Klaus ins Kino.
f Wenn es morgen nebelig ist, bleibt Tina zu Hause.

Exercise 29 (Unit 38): a möchte **b** Könnten **c** Würden
d Möchtest **e** hätte gern

Exercise 30 (Unit 38): a Würden Sie bitte das Fenster
schließen? **b** Könnten Sie mir bitte das Wort erklären? **c**
Würden Sie mir bitte ein Bier bringen? **d** Könnten Sie
einen Moment warten?

Exercise 31 (Unit 39): a Es ist ihr egal **b** Es tut mir weh.
c Es ist kalt. **d** Es tut mir Leid.

Exercise 32 (Unit 40): a an **b** fern **c** auf **d** statt
e ab **f** zurück

Exercise 33 (Unit 40): a Wir steigen in Düsseldorf um.
b Er fährt nach Hameln zurück. **c** Ich steige in der
Burgstraße aus. **d** Die Messe findet in Köln statt. **e** Ich
rufe dich morgen Abend an.

Exercise 34 (Unit 42): a hat **b** ist **c** sind **d** habe **e** ist

Exercise 35 (Unit 47): a Mercedes werden in Deutschland
produziert. **b** Computer werden in Japan produziert.
c Fernseher werden in den USA produziert. **d** Motorräder
werden in England produziert. **e** Ferraris werden in Italien
produziert. **f** Jeans werden in Taiwan produziert.
g Peugeots werden in Frankreich produziert.

Exercise 36 (Unit 52): a Der Pullover, den ich gekauft habe,
ist grün. **b** Das Hemd, das ich gekauft habe, ist gestreift.
c Die Bluse, die ich gekauft habe, ist schwarz. **d** Der
Mantel, den ich gekauft habe, ist braun. **e** Die Schuhe, die
ich gekauft habe, sind blau. **f** Die Hose, die ich gekauft
habe, ist schwarz.

Exercise 37 (Unit 56): a Die Katze sitzt **auf dem** Sessel.
b Die Katze ist **hinter dem** Sessel. **c** Die Katze springt **auf
den** Sessel. **d** Die Katze geht **hinter den** Sessel.

Exercise 38 (Unit 62): a groß, traurig und gut gebaut
b klein, schlank und hübsch; groß, schlank und freundlich

Exercise 39 (Unit 64): a neuen **b** intelligente **c** kleines **d** guten **e** alten

Exercise 40 (Unit 65): Schöne, helle 2 Zi. Wohnung; sehr ruhige Lage, separates Klo; große Küche; neues Bad; kleiner Keller

Exercise 41 (Unit 66): a Guten Abend! **b** Frohes Neues Jahr!/Guten Rutsch! **c** Herzlichen Glückwunsch zum Geburtstag! **d** Gute Nacht! **e** Schönes Wochenende! **f** Guten Appetit! **g** Guten Tag! **h** Vielen Dank

Exercise 42 (Unit 66): a Schöne Grüße, **b** Mit freundlichen Grüßen, **c** Schöne Grüße, **d** Mit freundlichen Grüßen

Exercise 43 (Unit 67): a 3 **b** 5 **c** 6 **d** 1 **e** 7 **f** 2 **g** 4

Exercise 44 (Unit 67): a Der Rhein ist länger als die Themse. Die Themse ist nicht so lang wie der Rhein. **b** Eine Maus ist kleiner als eine Katze. Eine Katze ist nicht so klein wie eine Maus. **c** Ein Porsche ist schneller als ein Mini. Ein Mini ist nicht so schnell wie ein Porsche. **d** Der Everest ist höher als Ben Nevis. Ben Nevis ist nicht so hoch wie der Everest. **e** England ist kälter als Australien. Australien ist nicht so kalt wie England. **f** Indien ist ärmer als Amerika. Amerika ist nicht so arm wie Indien. **g** Mein Bruder ist älter als ich. Ich bin nicht so alt wie mein Bruder.

Exercise 45 (Unit 69): a fährt am schnellsten. **b** arbeitet am besten. **c** kommt am spätesten. **d** wartet am längsten. **e** kocht am schlechtesten.

Exercise 46 (Unit 72): a Er hört jeden Tag Radio, während er frühstückt. **b** Ich gehe zum Arzt, wenn ich krank bin. **c** Er liest Zeitung, sobald er zu Hause ist. **d** Wir lernen Deutsch, weil wir nächstes Jahr nach Deutschland fahren.

Exercise 47 (Unit 81): a vierundvierzig dreiundzwanzig dreißig **b** elf siebenundvierzig sechsundfünfzig **c** einundachtzig null neun zwo(zwei)undsechzig **d** dreiundneunzig zwölf fünfundsiebzig

Exercise 48 (Unit 82): a vierzehntausendeinhundert **b** neuntausenddreihundert **c** siebentausend **d** sechstausendsechshundert **e** zweitausendsechshundert **f** dreitausendeinhundert **g** viertausendfünfhundert

Exercise 49 (Unit 83): a siebte achte **b** siebenundzwanzigste elfte **c** einunddreißigste siebte **d** vierzehnte **e** sechsundzwanzigste fünfte neunzehnhundertneunundfünfzig **f** dritte neunte neunzehnhundertsechsundsechzig

Exercise 50 (Unit 84): a zweimal **b** viermal **c** dreimal **d** fünfmal **e** einmal

Exercise 51 (Unit 85): a Heute ist der sechste Juli. **b** Heute ist der zwölfte Januar. **c** Heute ist der erste Mai. **d** Heute ist der dritte Oktober.

Exercise 52 (Unit 85): a vom ersten bis zum zehnten März
b vom neunzehnten bis zum fünfundzwanzigsten Juli
c vom dreißigsten November bis zum dritten Dezember

Exercise 53 (Unit 87): a sieben Stunden neunundzwanzig
Minuten und acht Sekunden **b** vier Stunden sechzehn
Minuten und achtunddreißig Sekunden **c** drei Stunden
vierundvierzig Minuten und zwölf Sekunden

accusative case The accusative case is used for the direct object in a sentence, e.g. **Dirk kauft <u>den Pullover</u>** *Dirk buys the pullover*. (See also **case**.)

adjective An adjective is a word which describes a noun, e.g. **Er ist <u>klein</u>** *He/It is small*, **eine <u>lange</u> Straße** *a long street*.

adverb An adverb describes a verb, e.g. **er fährt <u>langsam</u>** *he drives slowly*.

article See **definite article, indefinite article**.

case There are four cases in German: nominative, accusative, dative and genitive. Case shows the role of nouns in a sentence. The nouns, pronouns, articles, determiners and adjectives in a sentence change by taking endings in the different cases. (See also **nominative case, accusative case, genitive case, dative case**.)

clause See **main clause, subordinate clause**.

co-ordinating conjunction See **conjunction**.

comparative The comparative form of the adjective is used to make comparisons, e.g. **das Auto ist <u>schneller</u>** *the car is faster*. (See also **adjective**.)

compound noun A compound noun is made up of two or more nouns, e.g. **der Regenschirm = der Regen + der Schirm** (*umbrella*).

conjunction A conjunction is a linking word between two sentences or parts of a sentence, e.g. **und** *and*, **oder** *or*. After a co-ordinating conjunction, the word order in the sentence does not change. A subordinating conjunction sends the verb to the end of the clause, e.g. **<u>Als</u> ich nach Hause <u>kam</u>, ...** *When I came home ...*

dative case The dative case shows the indirect object of the sentence, e.g. **Ich gebe** <u>meiner Mutter</u> **ein Geschenk** *I give my mother a present./I give a present to my mother.* (See also **case**.)

definite article The definite article is the word for *the* (**der, die, das**).

determiner A determiner comes before a noun and tells you the gender of the noun and whether the noun is singular or plural. There are several types of determiner in German, such as the definite article, the indefinite article, the possessives and words such as **dieser** *this* and **welcher** *which*.

future tense The future tense describes something that will happen in the future, e.g. **ich werde gehen** *I will go.*

gender Gender refers to the categories which nouns are divided into. There are three genders in German: masculine, feminine and neuter. Nouns belong to one of these groups, e.g. **der Bahnhof** *station* is masculine; **die Küche** *kitchen* is feminine; **das Haus** *house* is neuter.

genitive case The genitive case shows possession, e.g. **das Auto** <u>des Mannes</u> *the man's car/the car of the man.* (See also **case**.)

imperative The imperative is the command form and is used for requests and instructions, e.g. **Sei ruhig!** *Be quiet!*

indefinite article The indefinite article is the word for *a* (**ein, eine, ein**).

infinitive The infinitive is the form of the verb you will find in the dictionary. Nearly all infinitives end in **-en** in German, e.g. **spiel<u>en</u>** *to play.*

inseparable verb Inseparable verbs have two parts, but the prefix does not separate from the rest of the verb, e.g. <u>be</u>zahlen *to pay*. (See also **separable verb**.)

interrogative An interrogative is a question word, e.g. **wer?** *who?*, **was?** *what?*

irregular verb There are a few irregular verbs in German, e.g. **haben** *to have* → **er hat** *he has*, **sein** *to be* → **ich bin** *I am*.

main clause A sentence has a main clause which contains a verb, e.g. **Er geht zur Arbeit.** *He goes to work.* (See also **subordinate clause**.)

mixed verb A small group of verbs are called mixed verbs. They change their stem in the past like strong verbs, but the past participle ends in -t like weak verbs, e.g. **bringen** *to bring* → **ich brachte** *I brought*.

modal verb Six verbs in German are called modal verbs: **dürfen, können, mögen, müssen, sollen** and **wollen**. They are used with other verbs to make requests, ask permission, etc.

nominative case The nominative case shows the subject of the verb in a sentence, e.g. <u>Der Mann</u> trinkt Wein. *The man is drinking wine.* (See also **case**.)

noun A noun is used to name or identify a person, an animal, a place or an idea, e.g. **eine Frau** *a woman*, **der Hund** *the dog*, **München** *Munich*, **die Idee** *the idea*. (See also **compound noun**, **weak noun**.)

past participle The past participle shows that something is completed, and is used together with other verbs in certain tenses, e.g. **ich habe** <u>gebaut</u> *I have built*. (See also **perfect tense**, **past perfect tense**.)

past perfect tense The past perfect tense, also known as the pluperfect tense, describes something that had happened before something else in the past, e.g. **ich war gegangen** *I had gone*.

perfect tense The perfect tense describes something that has happened in the past, e.g. **ich bin gegangen** *I have gone/I went*.

personal pronoun See **pronoun**.

pluperfect tense See **past perfect tense**.

plural See **singular** AND **plural**.

possessives Possessives show who something belongs to, e.g. **mein** *my*, **ihr** *her*: <u>mein</u> **Hund** *my dog*.

preposition Prepositions indicate the position of people or things, or indicate time, e.g. <u>in</u> **der Kirche** *in church*, <u>für</u> **eine Woche** *for a week*.

present tense The present tense describes what is going on now, e.g. **ich gehe** *I go/I'm going*.

pronoun A pronoun replaces a noun. A personal pronoun refers to a person or a thing, e.g. **ich** *I*, **du** *you*, **es** *it*. A relative pronoun expresses *who*, *which* or *that*, e.g. **das Haus**, <u>das</u> … *the house that/which* …

reflexive verb A reflexive verb describes a person or thing doing something to himself/herself/itself, e.g. **ich wasche mich** *I wash myself*.

regular verb See **weak verb**.

relative pronoun See **pronoun**.

reported speech See **subjunctive**.

separable verb Separable verbs have two parts. The prefix (at the front) separates from the rest of the verb and goes to the end of the sentence, e.g. <u>an</u>kommen: der Zug <u>kommt</u> <u>an</u> *the train arrives*.

simple past tense or **imperfect tense** The simple past tense describes something that happened in the past, e.g. **ich ging** *I went*.

singular and plural Singular refers to one person, thing, etc., e.g. **die Frau** *the woman*, **eine Katze** *a cat*; plural refers to more than one person, thing, etc., e.g. **die Männer** *the men*, **drei Taxis** *three taxis*.

stem See **verb stem**.

strong verb Strong verbs do not always follow a regular pattern. The stem often changes and they take different endings from **weak verbs** (except in the present tense), e.g. **fahren → er fährt, er fuhr** *he goes, he went*.

subjunctive The subjunctive form of the verb is used in conditions to express what might happen, e.g. **wenn ich Geld <u>hätte</u>** *if I had money*. It is used in some polite requests, e.g. **Ich <u>möchte</u> einen Kaffee** *I'd like a coffee*. It is also used in reported speech to report what someone said, e.g. **Er sagte, er <u>sei</u> in Rom.** *He said he was in Rome.*

subordinate clause A sentence can also have one or more subordinate clauses. This clause is introduced by a subordinating conjunction which sends the verb to the end, e.g. **Ich esse Schokolade, <u>weil ich Hunger habe</u>.** *I'm eating some chocolate because I'm hungry.*

subordinating conjunction See **conjunction**.

superlative The superlative form is used in comparisons to express *the most* or *the least* etc., e.g. der <u>höchste</u> Turm *the highest tower*. (See also **adjective, comparative**.)

tense Tense, e.g. present, past, future tense, indicates the time an action takes place. (See also **present tense, perfect tense, simple past tense, past perfect tense, future tense**.)

umlaut An umlaut is the two dots sometimes placed over the vowels a, o or u, e.g. er f<u>ä</u>hrt *he travels, drives*, die S<u>ö</u>hne *sons*, das B<u>ü</u>ro *office*.

verb Verbs describe actions, feelings and states, e.g. **gehen** *to go*, **denken** *to think*, **sein** *to be*.

verb stem The part of the infinitive without -en is called the stem. Verb endings are added to this stem, e.g. the stem of **kaufen** *to buy* is **kauf-**.

weak noun Some masculine (**der**) words add an -n or -en ending in certain cases. They are called weak nouns, e.g. **den Jungen** *the boy*, **den Elefanten** *the elephant*.

weak verb Most verbs in German are regular and are known as weak verbs. The stem of a weak verb does not change, e.g. **kaufen** → ich <u>kauf</u>e, ich <u>kauf</u>te *I buy, I bought*.

The symbol / shows a separable prefix.

die Anwältin (-nen) *lawyer (f.)*
der Arzt (¨e) *doctor*
auf/passen *to look after*
die Ausstellung (-en) *exhibition*

die Bäckerei (-en) *baker's*
das Bad (¨er) *bath(room)*
baden *to bathe, to swim*
die Bauchschmerzen *stomach ache*
der Bauernhof (¨e) *farm*
der Becher (-) *pot*
das Bein (-e) *leg*
der Berg (-e) *mountain*
der Besuch (-e) *visit*
besuchen *to visit*
das Bett (-en) *bed*
bleiben *to stay*
die Blume (-n) *flower*
die Bluse (-n) *blouse*
der Brief (-e) *letter*
die Briefmarke (-n) *stamp*

der Chef (-s) *boss*
die Cousine (-n) *(f.) cousin*

der Deutschkurs (-e) *German course*

die Dose (-n) *tin*
duschen *to have a shower*

entwickeln *to develop*
die Erbse (-n) *pea*
die Erdbeere (-n) *strawberry*
erklären *to explain*
das Essen (-) *meal*

die Fähre (-n) *ferry*
faul *lazy*
das Fernsehinterview (-s) *TV interview*
die Fete (-n) *party*
das Filmfest (-e) *film festival*
die Flasche (-n) *bottle*
die Friseurin (-nen) *(f.) hairdresser*
der Frühling (-e) *spring*
das Frühstück (-e) *breakfast*
der Fußballplatz (¨e) *football pitch*

die Galerie (-n) *gallery*
das Gebäude (-) *building*
gemischt *mixed*
der Geschäftsmann (¨er) *businessman*

die Geschichte (-n) *story, history*

die Geschwister *brothers and sisters*

das Getränk (-e) *drink*

das Glas (¨er) *glass, jar*

der Grafiker (-) *graphic designer*

die Großmutter (¨) *grandmother*

der Großvater (¨) *grandfather*

die Gruppe (-n) *group*

der Hafen (¨) *port*

das Hallenbad (¨er) *indoor pool*

die Halsschmerzen *sore throat*

hassen *to hate*

hell *light, bright*

der Honig *honey*

die Hose (-n) *trousers*

das Hühnerfrikassee (-s) *chicken fricassee*

die Kantine (-n) *canteen*

kaputt *broken*

die Karte (-n) *ticket, card*

der Käse (-) *cheese*

das Kaufhaus (¨er) *department store*

der/das Keks (-e) *biscuit*

der Keller (-) *cellar*

der Kellner (-) *waiter*

der Kinderspielplatz (¨e) *playground*

das Kleid (-er) *dress*

das Klo (-s) *loo, toilet*

das Kloster (-) *monastery*

die Kneipe (-n) *pub*

der Koch (¨e) *chef*

die Kolleginnen *female colleagues*

die Kommode (-n) *chest of drawers*

krank *ill*

das Krankenhaus (¨er) *hospital*

der Krimi (-s) *thriller*

der Kuchen (-) *cake*

die Küche (-n) *kitchen*

der Kühlschrank (¨e) *fridge*

der Kunde (-n) *customer*

die Lage (-n) *position*

das Lamm (¨er) *lamb*

der Mantel (¨) *coat*

der Markt (¨e) *market*

der Mechaniker (-) *mechanic*

das Meer (-e) *sea*

das Mehl (-e) *flour*
die Messe (-n) *trade fair*
mischen *to mix*
die Möbel (*pl.*) *furniture*
modisch *fashionable*
die Mütze (-n) *cap*

der Neffe (-n) *nephew*
der Nuss (-̈e) *nut*

das Obst *fruit*
der Onkel (-) *uncle*
der Ordner (-) *file*
der Osterhase (-n) *Easter bunny*

die Packung (-en) *packet*
der Palast (-̈e) *palace*
der Patient (-en) *patient*
das Portemonnaie (-s) *wallet*

die Rechnung (-en) *bill*
reden *to talk*
der Regenschirm (-e) *umbrella*
die Rinderroulade (-n) *rolled filled beef*
die Rückenschmerzen *backache*
ruhig *quiet, peaceful*
rühren *to whisk*

der Schal (-e) *scarf*

schälen *to peel*
das Schloss (-̈er) *castle, palace*
der Schlüssel (-) *key*
schneiden *to cut*
das Schuhgeschäft (-e) *shoe shop*
schwer *heavy, serious*
die Sonnenblume (-n) *sunflower*
der Spielplatz (-̈e) *playground*
das Spielzeug *toy*
das Stadtzentrum (-zentren) *town centre*
der Stift (-e) *pen*
der Stock (-̈e) *floor*
der Strand (-̈e) *beach*
die Straßenbahn (-n) *tram*
streichen *to paint*

die Tablette (-n) *tablet, pill*
die Tante (-n) *aunt*
die Teekanne (-n) *teapot*
das Telefonbuch (-̈er) *telephone directory*
der Teppich (-e) *carpet*
der Termin (-e) *appointment*
die Tochter (-̈) *daughter*
die Traube (-n) *grape*
das Tunesien *Tunisia*
der Turm (-̈e) *tower*

die Uhr (-n) *clock, watch*
der Unfall (⁻e) *accident*
untersuchen *to check*
der Urlaub (-e) *holiday*

verkaufen *to sell*
verpassen *to miss*
verzieren *to decorate*

der Weg (-e) *way*
die Wohnung (-en) *flat*

die Zahnschmerzen (*pl.*)
   toothache
die Zwillinge *twins*

Numbers in the index refer to units.